GUN
CARE
AND
REPAIR

GUN
CARE
AND
REPAIR

MONTE BURCH

Winchester Press

Library of Congress Cataloging in Publication Data

Burch, Monte.
  Gun care and repair.

  Includes index.
  1. Gunsmithing—Amateurs' manuals. I. Title.
TS535.B87   683'.4   78-2338
ISBN 0-87691-256-0

9 8 7 6 5 4 3 2 1

Published by Winchester Press
205 East 42nd Street
New York, N.Y. 10017

WINCHESTER is a Trademark of Olin Corporation
used by Winchester Press, Inc. under authority and
control of the Trademark Proprietor.

Printed in the United States of America

CONTENTS

ACKNOWLEDGMENTS

I would like to thank my dad for passing on his love of guns to me, as well as for giving me the opportunity to learn the skills necessary to work on them. I would also like to thank my wife, Joan, for all her support in helping me through the long night hours and hard spots that it takes to produce a book.

A special thanks to all the folks who have contributed photos, products, and just plain information and encouragement, including: Bob Brownell of Brownell's; Myron Barrie at Herter's; the Williams Gun Sight Company; Winchester-Western; Reinhart Fajen, Inc.; Chapman Manufacturing Company; B-Square Company; Birchwood Casey; W. R. Weaver Company; Redfield; Tasco; Bushnell Optical Company; Frank Mittermeier, Inc.; Simmons Gun Specialties, Inc.; Bausch & Lomb; Dremel Manufacturing Company; Robless Gun Safe; Gunline Tools; Safariland; Marlin; Savage; Remington; Weatherby; Sturm, Ruger; Smith & Wesson; Thompson/Center Arms; Benjamin Air Rifle Company; Browning; and Colt.

I would also like to thank *Workbench* Magazine and *Guns & Ammo* for letting me reprint some of my previously published material.

INTRODUCTION

Working on guns is a relaxing hobby that many people can enjoy. It is one of those hobbies that can be as simple or as complicated as you wish. Anyone who owns guns should take the time to learn their basic functions, not only so as to give them proper care, but for safety as well. There are also many times when gun work can be extremely frustrating—for instance, when you break off a screw head, or a soldering job doesn't hold, or you can't get a gun reassembled.

And that brings up another point. Anyone who says he has never had any problems reassembling a gun hasn't been there. I know professionals who have been stumped quite often. The problem is in the intense concentration required in this situation. Often it helps me to forget the problem for a while and come back later with a fresh outlook. I once wrestled with a disassembled bolt for a couple of hours and finally left it in disgust. A little later I happened to glance at it as I passed by and noticed the solution immediately. I had been hooking the safety in place on the wrong side, which was possible with that particular old-style bolt.

The main thing is to examine the problem carefully and slowly. Don't begin to hammer or beat on the gun to take it apart or get it back together. In most cases it won't go back together in that manner, and you'll ruin the gun and your temper as well. In fact, you'll often be surprised at how simple the job is once things begin to fall into place. I can only hope this book enables you to enjoy gun work as much as I do. Good luck!

GUN
CARE
AND
REPAIR

CHAPTER ONE

HOW GUNS WORK

The enjoyment of guns means a lot of different things to a lot of different folks. To some it means competitive games such as trap, skeet, or target-range shooting. It may also mean hunting duck, deer, quail, or other game. To many others, guns are items to collect for monetary as well as aesthetic reasons. Repairing, customizing, and caring for guns can also provide a challenging and interesting hobby. To be able to work on guns you must understand how they work and know basic safety rules. There are literally millions of different guns in the world, and it would be almost impossible to learn how each functions. You can, however, learn the basics of how the different types of actions work and why they work the way they do.

GUN SAFETY

Gun safety just can't be stressed enough. The rate of gun accidents is fortunately quite low compared to other accidents, but with proper safety rules most of these could be prevented. In addition to the standard safety rules that apply to shooters, gunsmiths and gun workers must also follow other gun-safety rules. If what you're doing is going to make the gun unsafe, or if it is unsafe to work on the gun in that manner, don't attempt it. There are several jobs that definitely should not be attempted by a beginning or home gunsmith, but should be

Make it an invariable habit to check a gun's action before handling it or passing it to someone else.

taken to a professional gunsmith who has the tools, skills, and knowledge. Most of these jobs are quite evident, and some of the less evident ones will be mentioned in this book.

Actually, basic safety rules are not complicated. They are easy to follow and few in number. Other than the basic rules, however, one very important thing must always be remembered: Anyone handling, shooting, or working with guns must maintain an attitude of seriousness and respect. At first this may require a conscious effort, but as time passes it becomes automatic and safety becomes instinctive.

1. Make sure the gun is unloaded. This is the cardinal rule and is obviously the most important first rule. More than one veteran shooter has experienced the disturbing sensation of discovering a shell in the chamber of a gun he thought was unloaded. Some guns are inherently more dangerous than others because it's

Keep guns locked up and ammunition stored separately in a locked cabinet.

hard or impossible to tell at a glance if they are loaded or not—for instance, an automatic pistol or shotgun. And this brings up the next rule.

2. Always open the action and check to make sure the gun is unloaded before examining it or handing it to someone else. You might gain a few friends this way instead of losing them. This should be done even if you're *sure* that a gun is unloaded. Among experienced gun handlers this is a kind of ritual that is repeated whenever a firearm is examined.

3. Always keep your gun properly cleaned and unloaded.

4. Never point a gun at anyone, and that includes yourself.

5. Always know the firepower of your gun and be sure of the target and backstop before firing.

6. When transporting guns, break them down if possible; remove clips, *make sure they're unloaded*, and place ammunition in a separate case.

7. Review your firearm storage facilities. Rifles and shotguns should be stowed securely in racks or cabinets, preferably locked. Handguns should be stored in a locked cabinet or drawer. Locked storage is particularly important if there are children in the home. Don't "hide" guns in closets or under your pillow. Children are curious and sooner or later they'll find them. If secure storage is not available, trigger locks or some other sort of locking safety device should be used. Breech locks are also recommended for rifles. Again, if there are children in the home, such locking devices are highly recommended.

8. Your last basic safety check should involve your ammunition storage. For complete safety, all ammunition should be kept under lock and key and in a location separate from your firearms. For an extra measure of safety, particularly with children in the home, store ammunition in another room or on a different floor level. The objective is to create a situation in which conscious effort is required to bring firearms and ammunition together. Obviously, the keys to all storage areas must be kept away from children.

9. The better you understand your guns, the safer you will be with them. To really understand a particular gun you should have a catalog sheet from the manufacturer. Many of these are still available for even the older guns. Or you might wish to purchase *The Encyclopedia of Modern Firearms,* an excellent reference book

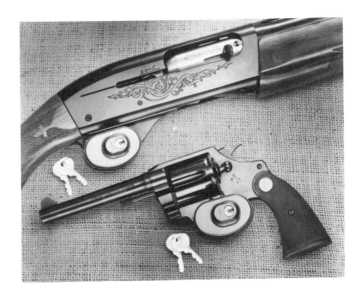

It's also a good idea to utilize trigger locks, particularly if you have small children in the house.

by Bob Brownell of Brownell's, Inc., Montezuma, Iowa: The NRA also has some excellent books and pamphlets on specific guns. Other good reference books from Winchester Press: *American Rifle Design and Performance, American Shotgun Design and Performance,* and *American Pistol and Revolver Design and Performance* by L. R. Wallack; *The Bolt Action: A Design Analysis,* by Stuart Otteson; *The .22 Rifle,* by Dave Petzal; and *The Accurate Rifle,* by Warren Page. All of these books can give you much more detailed information on specific guns than can be included here.

SHOTGUNS

There are basically five different types of shotguns: single-barrel, bolt-action, double-barrel, pump-action, and semi-automatic. Each has its advantages, its disadvantages, and its fan club.

Single-Barrel Shotguns

In shotgun parlance, "single-barrel" always means "single-shot," though the various repeating shotguns are, of course, also single-barrel. The single-barrel shotguns are naturally the simplest type of gun. Most of them, both the old-timers and the newer ones, have a "tip-up" method of breaking open. That is, the barrel is hinged at the rear to tip up for reloading. Although many of them were sold extremely cheaply, most of them were good strong guns. They utilize a bottom or underbolt system of locking that is operated by a lever on top of the gun. These were often called "farm guns" and when I was growing up almost every farmer around us had one of them for controlling the "polecats" and rats, as well as collecting a rabbit or two for the pot. In the smaller gauges they make a good starter gun for youngsters because of their safety factors in loading. They're easy to work on and economical, so the beginning gun worker can use one as a good practice gun. The only problem is finding parts for some of the older models.

Bolt-Action Shotguns

I started quail hunting as a boy with an old 20-gauge J. C. Higgins bolt-action shotgun, and became proficient enough to manage a few doubles on a covey rise. Today I don't get many more with a good double-barrel gun, but guess my reflexes

Savage-Stevens Single Barrel Shotgun
Model 94C and 94Y Series M
12, 16, 20 and .410 Gauge

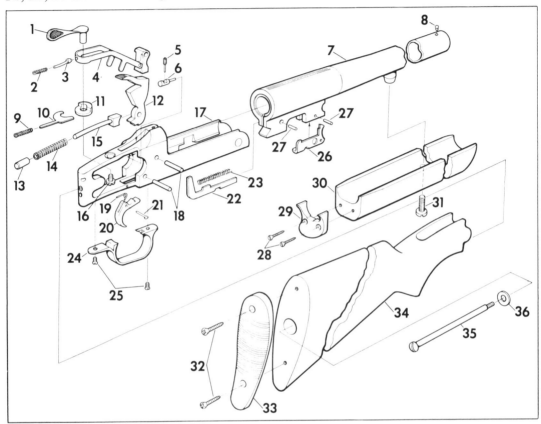

Exploded view of the Savage-Stevens single-barrel shotgun.

Key No.	Part Name	Key No.	Part Name
1	Top Snap	19	Trigger Spring
2	Locking Bolt Plunger Spring	20	Trigger
		21	Trigger Pin
3	Locking Bolt Plunger	22	Ejector
4	Locking Bolt Assembly	23	Ejector Spring
5	Firing Pin Screw	24	Trigger Guard
6	Firing Pin	25	Trigger Guard Screw
7	Barrel	26	Ejector Hook
8	Front Sight	27	Extractor & Ejector Pin
9	Top Snap Plunger Spring	28	Fore-end Iron Head Screw
10	Top Snap Plunger		
11	Top Snap Sleeve	29	Fore-end Pivot Plate
12	Hammer	30	Fore-end Wood
13	Mainspring Plunger Seat		Fore-end Assembly
14	Mainspring	31	Fore-end Screw
15	Mainspring Plunger Assembly	32	Butt Plate Screw
		33	Butt Plate
16	Top Snap Screw	34	Stock
17	Frame	35	Stock Bolt
18	Locking Bolt, Hammer Pin	36	Stock Bolt Washer

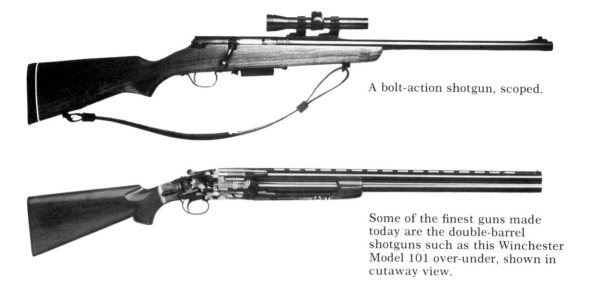

A bolt-action shotgun, scoped.

Some of the finest guns made today are the double-barrel shotguns such as this Winchester Model 101 over-under, shown in cutaway view.

have slowed down quite a bit. In fact, shooting too fast is one of the beginning quail hunter's problems, and the old bolt-action probably slowed down my young reflexes to the point that it made an ideal gun for me at the time.

Most of these shotguns were made quite cheaply, and as a result, very few older models are still in working order. Don't confuse them, however, with the newer slug and goose guns. These guns definitely have a purpose and are sturdy, well-made guns by reputable companies. Their operation is basically the same as that of a bolt-action rifle, which we will discuss later in the chapter.

Double-Barrel Shotguns

These are available in two forms: side-by-side and over-under. For years the double-barrel shotgun was the standard. Then came the pump and then the automatics, and the old doubles took back seat. But today we're seeing a resurgence of interest in double-barrel shotguns. One of the problems has been the cost of making these guns. Although their operation is quite simple, the mechanism utilizes many finely shaped and hand-fitted parts. Recently we have seen many fine imported doubles.

Double-barrel guns may utilize a single trigger or double selective triggers. They almost all break open by tripping the barrel down and away from the breech. Some of the finest guns made in the United States were the old Parker, L. C. Smith,

Regency
12 Gauge

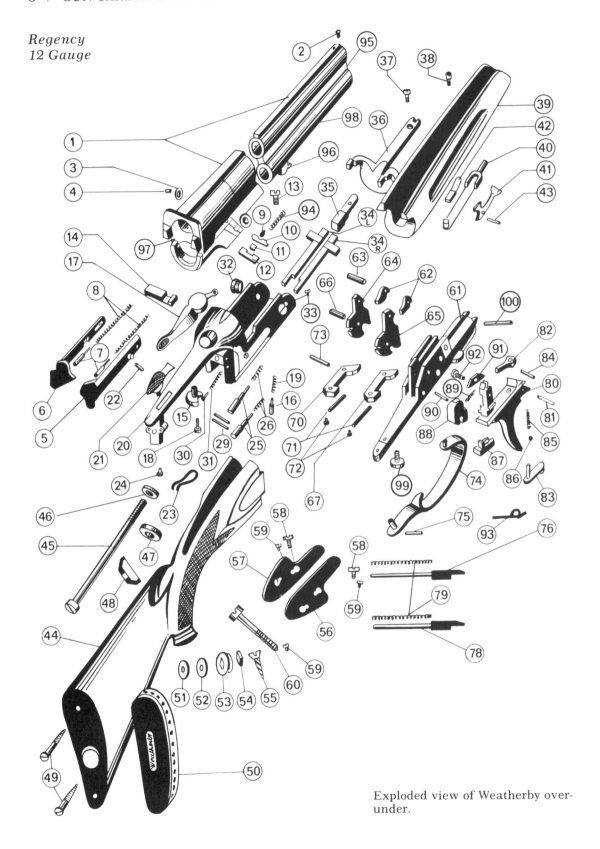

Exploded view of Weatherby over-under.

Key No.	Part Name	Key No.	Part Name	Key No.	Part Name
39	Forearm	97	Monobloc	25	Firing Pin
37	Retaining Screw, Rear	98	Barrel	26	Firing Pin Spring
38	Retaining Screw, Front	59	Locking Screw	24	Safety Spring Screw
35	Cocking-Rod Cam	58	Side Plate Screw	23	Safety Spring
36	Forearm Iron	60	Side Plate Bolt	22	Safety Pin
43	Latch Pin	56	Side Plate (Right)	21	Safety
42	Latch Spring	57	Side Plate (Left)	75	Trigger Guard Pin
41	Latch	44	Buttstock	74	Trigger Guard
40	Latch Housing	54	Diamond Inlay	99	Tang Screw
6	Top Ejector	55	No. 8 × 1" Wood Screw	100	Bottom Plate Pin
5	Bottom Ejector	53	Pistol Grip Cap	63	Cocking Cam Pin
7	Ejector Plunger	52	Spacer, White	62	Cocking Cam
8	Ejector Spring	51	Spacer, Black	66	Hammer Pin
13	Ejector Retainer Screw	45	Stockbolt	65	Hammer (Right)
12	Locking Bar Cover Plate (Right)	48	Split Ring	64	Hammer (Left)
12	Locking Bar Cover Plate (Left)	46	Lockwasher	73	Seal Pin
		47	Stockbolt Washer	67	Sear (Right)
10	Ejector Locking Bar (Right)	49	No. 8 × 1" Wood Screw	70	Sear (Left)
10	Ejector Locking Bar (Left)	50	Recoil Pad	72	Sear Spring Screw
		78	Mainspring Pilot (Right)	71	Sear Spring
94	Locking Bar, Tension Spring	76	Mainspring Pilot (Left)	81	Trigger Assembly Pin
		79	Mainspring	84	Selector Pin
11	Detent Cover Plate (Right)	34R	Cocking Rod (Right)	82	Selector
		34L	Cocking Rod (Left)	86	Steel Ball, 125 Dia.
11	Detent Cover Plate (Left)	18	Top Lever Screw	85	Selector Spring
9	Detent (Right)	17	Top Lever	83	Selector Lever
9	Detent (Left)	15	Top Lever Spring Return	90	Inertia Block Pin
2	Front Bead	31	Top Lever Spring	89	Inertia Block Spring
1	Ventilated Rib	30	Pilot Spring	88	Inertia Block
95	Side Rib	14	Crossbolt	87	Inertia Block Slide
96	Latch Hook	16	Crossbolt Detent	92	Inertia Block Cam Screw
4	Locking Screw	19	Detent Spring	93	Trigger Spring
3	Pivot Hinge	33	Locking Screw	91	Inertia Block Cam
		32	Pivot Plug	80	Trigger
		29	Firing Pin Retainer Pin	61	Bottom Plate

and Ithaca double-barrel guns. Many of these and similar old guns are still in good working shape today, although those with twist or Damascus barrels should be relegated to the wall, because they are unsafe with modern powders. There are a good number of old cheaper-model doubles around, and many of them should be considered unsafe because they are usually extremely loose. A good old solid side-by-side gun, however, can usually be picked up fairly economically and may need nothing more than a new firing pin or spring or a little stock or bluing work and you'll end up with a fine gun. The only problem is again that you may have to make parts for them. There are some very good side-by-sides on the market today, including the Winchester Model 21, a classic of the gunsmith's art, and the more economical Fox from Savage-Stevens, in addition to some of the better imported guns. Many of them are simple to work on because

Fox Model BDE, BSE-C, BSE-D, BSE-E, BSE
Series F and H
Double Barrel Shotgun With Automatic Ejectors

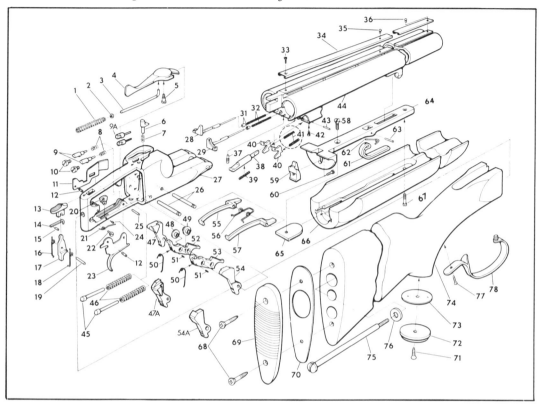

the side or bottom plates can be removed to show most of the working mechanism.

The over-under shotgun works on the same basic principle as the side-by-side, except the two barrels are placed one on top of the other. The one main disadvantage is that a over-under must be broken open much deeper to enable the bottom shell to be extracted. Over-unders cost a bit more than the side-by-sides and for several years they were practically the only double made in the United States.

Pump-Action Shotguns

The pump gun is a favorite gun with many hunters and shooters, mainly because of price, repeating capability, and reliability. Many of these old guns such as the Winchester Model 12 are not only still around, but providing reliable shooting as well. In use the shooter merely has to pull the fore-end back

Parts common to most models are listed below.
Exceptions follow general listing.

Key No.	Part Name	Key No.	Part Name	Key No.	Part Name
1	Top Snap Plunger Spring	28	Extractor (Left)	58	Fore-end Screw (Rear)
2	Top Snap Plunger Collar	29	Extractor (Right)	59	Ejector
3	Top Snap Plunger	31	Ejector Collar	60	Ejector Screw
4	Top Snap	32	Ejector Spring	61	Fore-end Spring
5	Top Snap Screw	33	Top Rib Lock Screw	62	Fore-end Spring Spring
6	Top Snap Trip	34	Top Rib	63	Fore-end Spring Pin
7	Top Snap Trip Spring	35	Rear Sight	64	Fore-end Iron
8	Firing Pin Spring	36	Front Sight	65	Fore-end Insert
9	Firing Pin	37	Extractor Screw	66	Fore-end Wood
10	Firing Pin Retaining Screw	38	Cocking Plunger	67	Fore-end Screw (Front)
11	Slide	39	Cocking Plunger Spring	68	Butt Plate Screw
12	Trigger Stud	40	Ejector Sear	69	Butt Plate
13	Safety Button	41	Ejector Sear Spring	70	Butt Plate Liner
14	Safety Spring	42	Cocking Plunger Retaining Screw	71	Pistol Grip Cap Screw
15	Safety Plunger	43	Ejector Sear Pin	72	Pistol Grip Cap
16	Slide Spring	44	Barrel	73	Pistol Grip Cap Liner
17	Safety Lever	45	Mainspring Plunger	74	Stock
18	Trigger Spring	46	Mainspring	75	Stock Bolt
19	Safety Lever Pin	47	Hammer (Left)	76	Stock Bolt Washer
20	Inertia Block	48	Cocking Lever Spacer	77	Trigger Guard Screw
21	Inertia Block Spring	49	Cocking Lever Bushing	78	Trigger Guard
22	Inertia Block Spring Screw	50	Cocking Lever Spring		
23	Trigger	51	Cocking Lever Spring Pin		*Parts for models BSE-C, D, E,*
24	Inertia Block Pin	52	Cocking Lever (Left)		*Series F and H only*
25	Trigger Pin	53	Cocking Lever (Right)	9A	Firing Pin
26	Sear, Cocking Lever and Hammer Pin	54	Hammer (Right)	47A	Hammer (Left)
27	Frame	55	Sear (Left)	54A	Hammer (Right)
		56	Sear Spring		
		57	Sear (Right)		

Cutaway view of Winchester
Model 1200 pump shotgun.

to eject the spent shell and feed another into the
chamber. A good experienced pump-gun shooter
can shoot almost as fast as a shooter with an automatic gun. One of the main problems with pump
guns is that the one single barrel doesn't allow for
the instant choke selection one has with the double-barrel guns. However, an adjustable choke installed on the gun barrel makes selection possible
in advance of the shots.

There are a good number of old pump guns
around, such as the Winchester Model 12, which

Savage Models 30J, K, T and Series A, B and C
Takedown Repeating Slide-Action Shotgun
12 and 20 Gauge

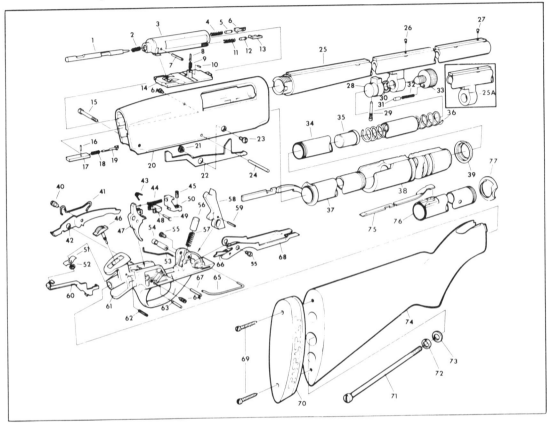

Exploded view of Savage Model
30 pump shotgun.

make great working guns for the home gun worker. Normally the only thing that will be needed is maybe a new blue job and some stockwork. Some may also need to be tightened up a bit.

Autoloading Shotguns

"Automatics," as they are called, are not really automatics, but semi-automatics; the more precise term is "autoloader." These guns are a favorite with many shooters, mostly because of the ease of firing more than one shot. Merely pulling the trigger each time you wish to fire does the trick. The spent shell is ejected and the new one brought into the chamber by either the recoil from the gun or some of the gas from the previously fired shell.

The recoil system utilizes the force of a spring-loaded moving barrel. When the trigger is pulled in the recoil system, the recoil forces the barrel and breechblock, which are locked together, rearward.

Parts common to most models are listed below.
Exceptions follow general listing.

Key No.	Part Name	Key No.	Part Name	Key No.	Part Name
1	Firing Pin	28	Magazine Plug	54	Hammer Bushing
2	Firing Pin Spring	29	Magazine End Plug	55	Lifter Screw
3	Breech Bolt		Screw	56	Mainspring Plunger
4	Extractor Spring (Left)	30	Takedown Screw	57	Mainspring
5	Extractor Plunger (Left)		Retaining Ring	58	Hammer
6	Extractor (Left)	31	Takedown Screw	60	Safety Lever
6A	Ejector Screw		Plunger	61	Trigger Guard
7	Firing Pin Stop Pin	32	Takedown Screw	62	Safety Lever Retaining
8	Firing Pin Retractor		Plunger Spring		Pin
	Plunger	33	Takedown Screw	63	Trigger Pin
9	Firing Pin Retractor	34	Magazine Tube	64	Safety Adjustment Screw
	Spring	35	Magazine Follower	65	Lifter Spring
10	Firing Pin Retractor	36	Magazine Spring	66	Lifter Pawl
	Plunger Pin	37	Operating Handle Bar	67	Sear Pin
11	Extractor Spring (Right)		Assembly	68	Lifter Assembly
12	Extractor Plunger	38	Operating Handle Wood	69	Recoil Pad Screw
	(Right)	39	Operating Handle Collar,	70	Recoil Pad
13	Extractor (Right)		Front	71	Stock Bolt
14	Slide Assembly	40	Slide Lock Spring Stud	72	Stock Bolt Lock Washer
15	Trigger Guard Screw	41	Slide Lock Spring	73	Stock Bolt Washer
16	Ejector Pin	42	Slide Lock Assembly	74	Stock
17	Ejector Assembly	43	Sear Trip Spring		
18	Ejector Spring	44	Trigger Spring	*Parts for Model 30*	
19	Ejector Plunger	45	Sear Engagement Screw	*Series C only*	
20	Receiver	46	Safety	75	Operating Handle Bar
21	Cartridge Stop Pivot Nut	47	Trigger	76	Operating Handle Tube
22	Cartridge Stop	48	Sear Trip		Assembly
23	Cartridge Stop Pivot	49	Sear Trip Pin	77	Operating Handle Collar,
	Screw	50	Sear		Rear
24	Trigger Guard Pin	51	Safety Spring		
25	Barrel	52	Safety Retainer Ring		
26	Rear Sight	53	Slide Lock Release		
27	Front Sight		Spring		

As the barrel and breechblock reach the rear position, the bolt then releases the barrel and it slams forward. At the same time the empty shell is carried forward and ejected and a new shell is picked up and fed into the chamber. As soon as the breechblock reaches the breech of the barrel, it is locked and the cycle is complete; the gun is ready to fire again. This may be called a long-recoil system or short-recoil system depending on the distance the barrel moves to complete the cycle.

The gas-operated automatic utilizes much the same action except that the barrel doesn't move; many shooters just can't get used to the moving barrel of a recoil-system automatic. In this case a small hole in the barrel allows a tiny bit of gas to escape from the fired shell into a piston arrangement. This piston moves a rod to unlock the breechblock and allow it to move to the rear, carrying the spent casing. This is then ejected out the

Centurion Automatic

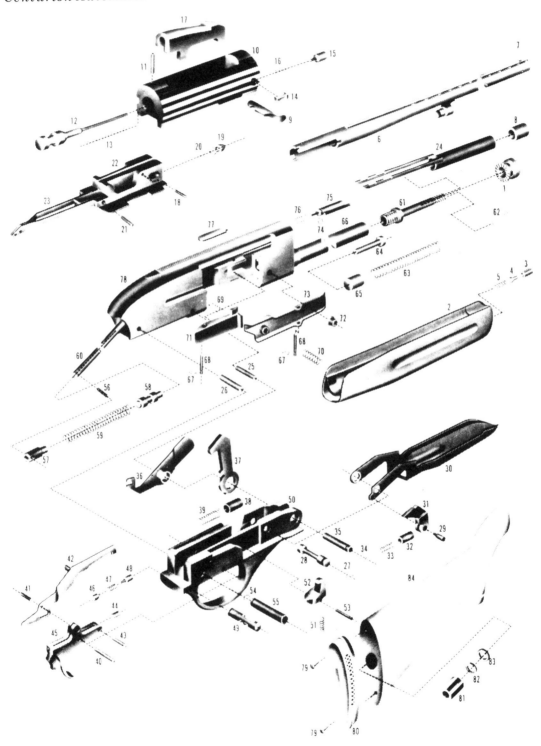

Exploded view of Weatherby
Centurion automatic shotgun.

Key No.	Part Name	Key No.	Part Name	Key No.	Part Name
1	Fore-end Cap	28	Lifter Pivot	57	Action Tube Plug
2	Forearm	29	Lifter Dog Pin	58	Action Tube Follower
3	Fore-end Cap Plunger Guide	30	Lifter	59	Action Tube Spring
		31	Lifter Dog	60	Action Tube
4	Fore-end Cap Plunger	32	Dog Follower	61	Magazine Extension
5	Plunger Spring	33	Dog Follower Spring	62	Extension Retainer
6	Barrel Assembly	34	Detent Spring	63	Magazine Spring
7	Barrel Bead	35	Hammer Pivot Tube	64	Magazine Plug
8	Gas Piston	36	Lockshaft Assembly	65	Magazine Follower
9	Operating Handle	37	Hammer	66	Magazine Tube
10	Bolt	38	Hammer Plunger	67	Latch Pin Retainer
11	Retaining Pin	39	Hammer Plunger Spring	68	Latch Pin
12	Firing Pin	40	Trigger Pin	69	Latch Spring
13	Firing Pin Spring	41	Disconnector Pin	70	Blocker Spring
14	Extractor	42	Disconnector	71	Feed Latch
15	Extractor Plunger	43	Trigger Spring Pin	72	Bolt Release Button
16	Extractor Spring	44	Trigger Spring	73	Blocker Assembly
17	Locking Block	45	Trigger	74	Ejector Retainer
18	Retaining Pin	46	Retainer Screw	75	Ejector
19	Carrier Plunger	47	Safety Spring	76	Ejector Spring
20	Plunger Spring	48	Safety Plunger	77	Insert
21	Carrier Extension Pin	49	Safety Button	78	Housing
22	Carrier	50	Trigger Frame	79	Wood Screw
23	Extension Assembly Carrier	51	Sear Spring	80	Recoil Pad
		52	Sear	81	Action Tube Nut
24	Slide Assembly	53	Sear Pin	82	Action Tube Lockwasher
25	Front Trigger Frame Pin	54	Detent Spring	83	Buttstock Washer
26	Rear Trigger Frame Pin	55	Rear Trigger Frame Tube	84	Buttstock Subassembly
27	Retaining Ring	56	Action Tube Plug Pin		

Cutaway view of Winchester
Super-X semi-automatic shotgun.

ejection and loading port in the side of the receiver. The gun is cocked for the next shot, a fresh shell is picked up, and the breech goes forward back into position, readying the gun for the next shot. Sounds complicated, but a little time spent examining the gun and working the action will very quickly make it clear to you.

Like the pump gun, one of the disadvantages of this type of gun is the lack of choke selection during shooting. One of the most common problems with these guns is dirty or fouled actions. To work properly, the action of autoloaders should be kept as clean as possible and lubricated just enough to work properly. Often a stubborn autoloader can be made to work again by merely cleaning thoroughly as mentioned in Chapter Three then relubricating properly.

One of the common gunsmithing chores in both

automatics and pump shotguns is fitting or refitting a plug in the magazine to limit capacity to no more than two shells in the magazine and one in the chamber, as is required by the Federal Migratory Bird Treaty Act, as well as by some state laws. Although these plugs can be purchased from gun dealers, you can readily make one out of a dowel. Merely cut the dowel to 6 inches long and round the edges so it will slide freely and easily down in the magazine.

Cleanliness and lubrication are very important to an automatic shotgun. Here's what Remington says for their Model 1100 Automatic Shotgun:

"LUBRICATION—In normal usage, the Model 1100 requires very little lubrication. If action and gas mechanism parts are kept reasonably clean and free from excessive shooting residue, all that is necessary is a light film of oil to prevent the possibility of rusting. During extended periods of shooting, more frequent cleaning may be required—particularly parts of the gas mechanism. Overlubrication should be avoided at all times. If gun is to be stored for a period of time it should be carefully and thoroughly oiled. Outside surfaces should be wiped with oil occasionally. When gun is to be fired after being stored, all excess lubrication should be removed. The outside of your gun should be wiped with oil to prevent rust. Invisible 'prints' of moisture can cause rusting unless removed. Exposure to unfavorable weather or moisture from condensation also require additional care.

"BELOW FREEZING WEATHER—Special attention should be taken that oil is removed from action parts. If a lubricant is desired, use dry graphite or similar noncongealing lubricant. Take care also to prevent rusting from condensation and wetness (cold weather to warm room temperature) on action parts and barrel bore, barrel chamber."

RIFLES

Like shotguns, rifles are usually designated by the types of action they utilize. There are basically six different rifle styles: single-shot, tip-up, pump-action, bolt-action, lever-action, and semi-automatic or autoloader.

Single-Shot Rifles

There are a great number of the old single-shot

Savage Models 72 and 74
Single Shot
.22 Caliber Rifle

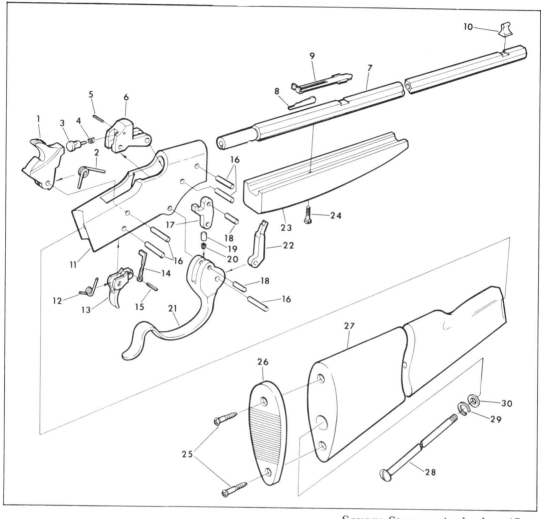

Savage-Stevens single-shot rifle.

Key No.	Part Name	Key No.	Part Name
1	Hammer	16	Hammer Pin
2	Hammer Spring	17	Link
3	Firing Pin	18	Link Pin
4	Firing Pin Spring	19	Detent Plunger
5	Firing Pin Securing Pin	20	Detent Plunger Spring
6	Breech Block	21	Lever
7	Barrel	22	Extractor
8	Rear Sight Step	23	Fore-end
9	Rear Sight	24	Fore-end Screw
10	Front Sight	25	Butt Plate Screws
11	Frame	26	Butt Plate
12	Trigger Spring	27	Stock
13	Trigger	28	Stock Bolt
14	Hammer Block	29	Stock Bolt Washer
15	Hammer Block Pin	30	Stock Bolt Lock Washer

Savage Models 110 C, D, DE and H
Repeating Bolt-Action Rifle
Right and Left Hand

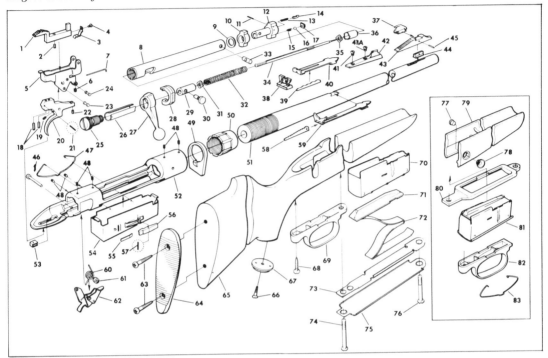

Exploded view of Savage Model
110 bolt-action rifle.

rifles around, basically because of their simple actions, which include the rolling-block, falling-block, and drop-block styles. One of the most famous of these old guns was the old-time Stevens Crackshot .22 rifle, a favorite with many a farm youngster. Other famous guns of this type include the Winchester single-shot (the same design rifle is manufactured today by Browning) and the famous Sharps and Ballard guns. Of the single-shot rifles manufactured today the Ruger and the Stevens Crackshot by Savage are pretty popular. Operation of these guns is simple and working on them can be a joy, but you'll probably have to make any parts you might need for the older models.

Tip-Up Rifles
This action is very similar to the action on tip-up shotguns. The breech actually tips up and away from the block, allowing you to remove or insert a

Parts common to most models are listed below.
Exceptions follow general listing.

Key No.	Part Name	Key No.	Part Name	Key No.	Part Name
1	Safety	28	Rear Baffle	64	Butt Plate
2	Trigger Pull Adjusting	29	Cocking Piece	65	Stock
	Screw	30	Cocking Piece Pin	66	Pistol Grip Cap Screw
3	Safety Detent Spring	31	Cocking Piece Link	67	Pistol Grip Cap
4	Safety Detent Spring		Washer	68	Trigger Guard Screw
	Screw	32	Mainspring	69	Trigger Guard
5	Trigger Bracket	33	Bolt Head Retaining Pin	70	Magazine Box
6	Trigger Pull Adjusting	34	Firing Pin	71	Magazine Follower
	Screw	35	Firing Pin Stop Nut	72	Magazine Spring
7	Trigger Pull Adjusting		Washer	73	Floor Plate Insert
	Spring	36	Firing Pin Stop Nut	74	Floor Plate Screw, Rear
8	Bolt Body	37	Front Sight	75	Floor Plate
9	Front Baffle Friction	38	Rear Sight (Folding)	76	Floor Plate Screw, Front
	Washer	43	Front Sight Base		
10	Front Baffle	44	Front Sight Dovetail		*Parts for Model 110C only*
11	Ejector Retaining Pin		Block	77	Magazine Latch Button
12	Bolt Head	45	Front Sight Pin	78	Escutcheon
13	Ejector Spring	46	Sear Pin	79	Stock
14	Ejector	47	Magazine Retainer	80	Floor Plate
15	Extractor Spring		Spring	81	Magazine Assembly
16	Steel Ball	48	Dummy Screw	82	Trigger Guard
17	Extractor	49	Recoil Lug	83	Magazine Ejector Spring
18	Trigger Travel Adjusting	50	Barrel Lock Nut		
	Screw	51	Barrel		*Parts for Model 110DE only*
19	Trigger Pin Retaining	52	Receiver	39	Rear Sight Step
	Screw	53	Trigger Pull Adjusting	40	Rear Sight
20	Trigger		Screw Cover	41	Front Sight Screw, Short
21	Trigger Spring Pin	54	Magazine Guide	41A	Front Sight Screw, Long
22	Trigger Engagement	55	Magazine Latch Spring	42	Front Sight
	Adjusting Screw	56	Magazine Latch		
23	Trigger Pin	57	Magazine Latch Pin		
24	Safety Bearing Pin	60	Sear Spring		
25	Bolt Assembly Screw	61	Sear Bushing		
26	Cocking Piece Sleeve	62	Sear		
27	Bolt Handle	63	Butt Plate Screw		

new shell. Most of these are top-lock actions and are broken open by moving a small lever on top of the gun near the hammer. Savage-Stevens still makes a few of these actions in their rifle-shotgun combination guns, as does Ithaca.

Bolt-Action Rifles

The bolt action is one of the simplest of rifle actions. There are basically two types of bolt actions. The first, based on the Mauser action, utilizes a T-shaped bolt and handle. The handle is first raised, then the bolt is pulled back to open the action, eject a shell, and insert a new one. The second kind is the straight-pull bolt often seen on small-caliber rifles. Simply pulling back against a spring operates the bolt; a mechanism inside the bolt does the turning and locking. Although there may be some minor differences, this is how a typical bolt-action rifle works:

Cutaway view of Winchester
Model 70 bolt-action rifle.

1. After firing the gun, raise the handle of the
bolt (in most cases 90°, sometimes less). This
allows the locking lugs to disengage from their
recesses in the front of the receiver. At the same
time the bolt is forced back just a bit, breaking
the spent casing from the chamber.

2. Pulling back on the bolt pulls the casing from
the chamber; the extractor hook holds the casing against the face of the bolt.

3. As soon as the bolt reaches the rear position,
an ejector contacts the left-hand side of the cartridge and flings it out of the gun.

4. The gun has been cocked during the first rais-
ing of the bolt handle.

5. As the bolt is pushed forward, the bottom of
it will engage the next cartridge, which is held
up against the bolt by the magazine spring. The
new cartridge is then pushed in place into the
chamber and seated against the face of the bolt.

6. Turning the handle of bolt down then makes
the locking lugs reengage the recesses of the receiver ring, allowing the cartridge to be firmly
locked in place and ready to fire.

Almost all of today's rifle manufacturers have a
line of bolt-actions, and these along with the older
models and the older military models, such as the
Mauser, Springfield, Enfield, etc., provide a
"playground" of guns for the amateur gun worker.
There are a great many things that can be done to
these guns to accurize or customize them. This
will be discussed in later chapters.

Lever-Action Rifles

The most famous of these guns are probably the
Winchester saddle guns of the old West. This action is still a mighty popular type with Winchester,
Marlin, and Savage, although the Savage guns
utilize a concealed hammer, often called a
"hammerless" model. These guns are typically the
hardest for the beginner to work on because most

*Savage Model 99 CD Series A
Repeating Lever-Action Rifle*

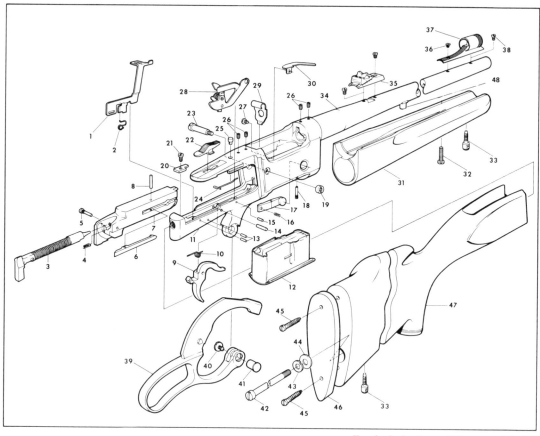

Exploded view of Savage Model
99 lever-action rifle.

Key No.	Part Name	Key No.	Part Name	Key No.	Part Name
1	Safety Slide	16	Magazine Latch Spring	34	Barrel
2	Safety Slide Spring	17	Magazine Latch	35	Rear Sight Assembly and Screws
3	Hammer Assembly	18	Magazine Latch Pin	36	Front Sight Screw, Short
4	Hammer Retractor Spring	19	Sear Screw Nut	37	Front Sight Assembly and Screws
5	Hammer Bushing Screw	20	Breech Bolt Stop		
6	Extractor	21	Breech Bolt Stop Screw	38	Front Sight Screw, Long
7	Breech Bolt	22	Safety Button	39	Lever
8	Extractor Pin	23	Sear Screw	40	Lever Bushing Screw
9	Trigger	24	Hammer Indicator Spring	41	Lever Bushing
10	Trigger Spring	25	Hammer Indicator No. 2	42	Stock Bolt
11	Receiver	26	Dummy Screw	43	Stock Bolt Lock Washer
12	Magazine Assembly	27	Ejector Screw	44	Stock Bolt Washer
13	Safety Slide Stop and Spring Pin	28	Sear Bracket Assembly	45	Recoil Pad Screw
		29	Filler Block	46	Recoil Pad
14	Trigger Pin	30	Ejector	47	Stock Assembly
15	Sear Bracket Pin	31	Fore-end	48	Barrel Stud
		32	Fore-end Screw		
		33	Swivel Stud		

Cutaway view of Winchester
Model 94 lever-action rifle.

of their mechanisms are concealed and fairly inaccessible and are held in place by pins or springs.
Unless you have a good manufacturers' drawing
and are willing to go carefully, you may lose parts
during disassembly, or not be able to figure out
their exact places during reassembly.

The Winchester ejects the shells out the top, the
Marlin type ejects them out the side.

Autoloading Rifles
The advantage of these rifles is that you can fire

Savage Models 6J, JDL, M, N, P
Stevens and Springfield 87J, M, N, and 187J, M, N
Automatic Repeating Rifles

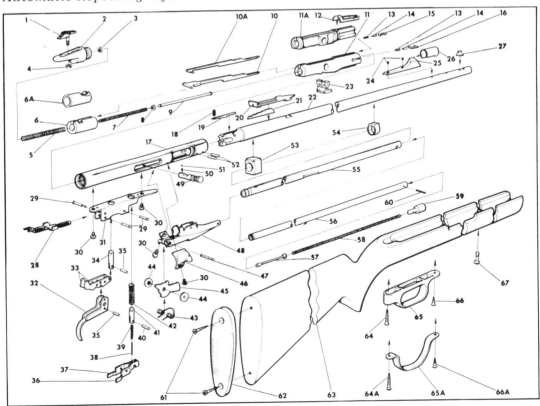

Exploded view of Savage Model
6J autoloading rifle.

them as fast as you can pull the trigger. They're often called "automatics," but they are really semi-automatic. One or two of the older models utilize recoil to eject the spent shell and insert the new one. However, most autoloaders, especially the modern ones manufactured today, utilize a gas system much like that of autoloading shotguns. The low-power .22s utilize the gas against a spring, whereas the more powerful high-caliber guns utilize the gas against a piston, as does an autoloader shotgun.

Again, like the shotgun, the recoil-operating guns are further broken down into long-recoil and short-recoil depending on how far the barrel moves in the action. For short recoil, the barrel normally won't move more than $\frac{1}{8}$ to $\frac{1}{2}$ inch. Then there is the blowback system invented by John Browning. It was in effect a simple gas system depending on

Parts common to most models listed below.
Exceptions follow general listing.

Key No.	Part Name	Key No.	Part Name	Key No.	Part Name
1	Safety Button	31	Release Housing	58	Magazine Follower Spring
2	Recoil Plug Assembly	32	Trigger		
3	Hammer Spring Washer	33	Release Lever	59	Magazine Plug
4	Safety Button Retaining Ring	34	Release Plunger	60	Magazine Plug Pin
		35	Trigger and Detent Plunger Pin	61	Butt Plate Screw
5	Hammer Spring			62	Butt Plate
6	Hammer	36	Detent Lever (Right)	63	Stock
7	Breech Bolt Spring	37	Detent Lever (Left)	64	Trigger Guard Screw (long)
8	Breech Bolt Spring Washer	38	Detent Plunger Inner Spring	64A	Trigger Guard Screw (long)
9	Breech Bolt Spring Rod	39	Detent Plunger Spring		
10	Firing Pin	40	Release Plunger Pin	65	Trigger Guard
11	Breech Bolt	41	Detent Plunger	65A	Trigger Guard
13	Extractor Plunger Spring	42	Release Spring	66	Trigger Guard Screw(short)
14	Extractor Plunger	43	Lifter Spring		
15	Extractor (Left)	44	Lifter Spacer	66A	Trigger Guard Screw (short)
16	Extractor (Right)	45	Lifter		
17	Receiver	46	Deflector	67	Takedown Screw
18	Bumper Spring	47	Lifter Pin		
19	Bumper	48	Magazine Guide		*Parts for Models 6J, M-87J*
20	Rear Sight	49	Locking Bolt		*M-187J, M only*
21	Rear Sight Step	50	Locking Bolt Plunger Ball Spring	6A	Hammer
22	Barrel			10A	Firing Pin
24	Front Sight Screw	51	Locking Bolt Plunger Ball	11A	Breech Bolt
25	Front Sight			12	Extractor
28	Safety Slide	52	Barrel Pin	27	Front Sight
29	Trigger, Detent and Release Lever Pin	53	Magazine Mount, rear		
		54	Magazine Mount, front		*Parts for Model 6P only*
30	Release Housing and Magazine Guide Screw	55	Outside Magazine Tube	23	Rear Sight
		56	Inside Magazine Tube	26	Front Sight Hood
		57	Magazine Follower		

Savage Model 170
Springfield Model 174
Slide-Action Rifles

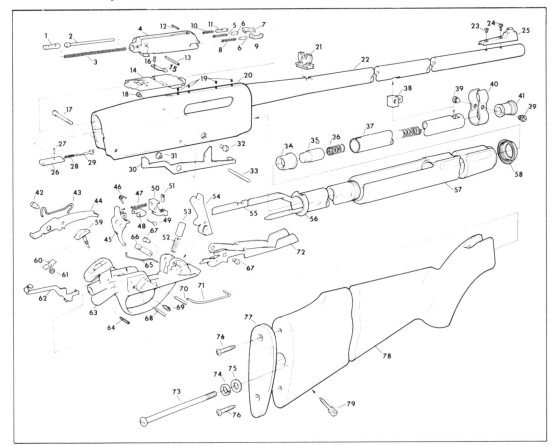

the inertia of the force against the breechblock. It was normally used on cartridges with low chamber pressure, although Winchester manufactured two large-caliber blowback rifles, in 1907 and 1910. One of the problems with this type of system is the weighting of the breechblock to keep it closed until the bullet is fired, an especially bad problem with heavy calibers. Often someone tries to use *standard*-velocity .22 Long Rifle cartridges in a .22 Long Rifle *high*-velocity chamber. With the blowback .22 semi-auto it just won't work, because the action isn't weighted for the extra push needed to operate the breechblock. These guns can be a bit tricky for the amateur to work on because they must be balanced and timed perfectly in order to operate properly.

Key No.	Part Name	Key No.	Part Name	Key No.	Part Name
1	Firing Pin Extension	31	Cartridge Stop Pivot Nut	56	Operating Handle Collar, Rear
2	Firing Pin	32	Cartridge Stop Pivot Screw	57	Operating Handle Wood
3	Firing Pin Spring	33	Trigger Guard Pin	58	Operating Handle Collar, Front
4	Breech Bolt	34	Magazine Tube Adapter		
5	Extractor Spring (Left)	35	Magazine Follower	59	Safety
6	Extractor Plunger	36	Magazine Spring	60	Safety Spring
7	Extractor (Left)	37	Magazine Tube	61	Safety Retaining Ring
8	Extractor Spring (Right)	38	Filling Block	62	Safety Lever
9	Extractor (Right)	39	Magazine Tube Yoke Screw	63	Trigger Guard
10	Shell Stop Spring	40	Magazine Tube Yoke	64	Safety Lever Retaining Pin
11	Shell Stop	41	Magazine Plug	65	Slide Lock Release Spring
12	Shell Stop Retaining Pin	42	Slide Lock Spring Stud		
13	Firing Pin Stop Pin	43	Slide Lock Spring	66	Hammer Bushing
14	Slide Assembly	44	Slide Lock and Spring Assembly	67	Lifter Screw
15	Bolt Support Spring			68	Trigger Pin
16	Bolt Support Spring Rivet	45	Trigger	69	Safety Adjusting Screw
17	Trigger Guard Screw	46	Sear Trip Spring	70	Sear Pin
18	Ejector Screw	47	Trigger Spring	71	Lifter Spring
19	Dummy Screw	48	Sear Trip	72	Lifter Assembly
20	Receiver	49	Sear Trip Pin	73	Stock Bolt
21	Rear Sight	50	Sear	74	Stock Bolt Lock Washer
22	Barrel	51	Sear Engagement Screw	75	Stock Bolt Washer
23	Front Sight Screw, Short	52	Mainspring	76	Butt Plate Screw
24	Front Sight Screw, Long	53	Mainspring Plunger	77	Butt Plate
25	Front Sight	54	Hammer Assembly	78	Stock Assembly
26	Ejector Assembly	55	Operating Handle Bar Assembly	79	Swivel Stud
27	Ejector Pin				
28	Ejector Spring				
29	Ejector Plunger				
30	Cartridge Stop				

Pump-Action Rifles

A pump-action or slide-action rifle works in much the same manner as the slide pump shotgun. Years ago the .22 pump gun was one of the most popular rifles on the market, although some writers will argue that the bolt-action has always been more popular. Today there aren't many being made, probably because of the popularity of the .22 automatic. One of the problems with pump guns is that they don't have the positive locking action of the bolt-action rifles. They weren't normally made in the larger calibers; however, the Remington 760 is a modern pump rifle that can be had in .270, .30-06, and .308. It has a turning-bolt locking system that is quite strong. Problems you'll often find with the older pump rifles are jamming or poor extraction and a general overall looseness. However, they're quite easy to work on for even the first-timer, and a bit of tightening and tuning can often result in a pretty good gun. They're also quite economical, except for some of the older collectible models.

Smith & Wesson
.38 Military & Police Revolver
Model No. 10

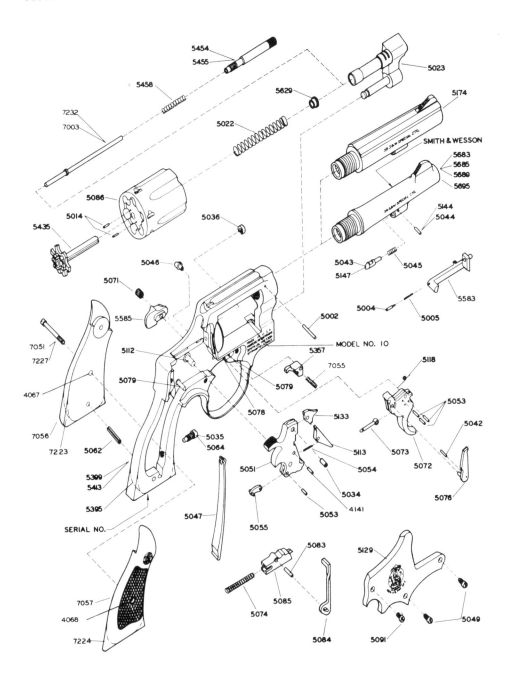

Key No.	Part Name	Key No.	Part Name	Key No.	Part Name
4067	Escutcheon	5073	Trigger Lever	5413	Frame for heavy barrel only
4068	Escutcheon Nut	5074	Rebound Slide Spring		
4141	Sear Pin	5076	Hand	5435	Extractor
5002	Barrel Pin	5078	Trigger Stud	5454	Extractor Rod for guns with 2″ barrels
5004	Bolt Plunger	5079	Cylinder Stop Stud		
5005	Bolt Plunger Spring	5079	Rebound Slide Stud	5455	Extractor Rod for guns with barrels over 2″
5014	Extractor Pin	5083	Rebound Slide Pin		
5022	Extractor Spring	5084	Hammer Block	5458	Center Pin Spring
5023	Yoke	5085	Rebound Slide	5488	Stock Screw, round butt
5034	Hammer Nose Rivet	5086	Cylinder, with extractor pins & gas ring	5583	Bolt
5035	Strain Screw, round butt			5585	Thumbpiece
5036	Hammer Nose Bushing	5091	Plate Screw, flat head	5599	Stock Screw, P.C.
5042	Hand Pin	5112	Hammer Stud	5629	Extractor Rod Collar
5043	Locking Bolt for guns with barrels over 2″	5113	Sear	5683	Barrel 2″
		5118	Hand Spring	5685	Barrel, 4″
5044	Locking Bolt Pin	5129	Side Plate	5689	Barrel, 5″
5045	Locking Bolt Spring	5133	Hammer Nose	5695	Barrel, 6″
5046	Frame Lug	5144	Locking Bolt Pin for heavy bbl.	7003	Center Pin for guns with barrels over 2″
5047	Mainspring				
5049	Plate Screw, crowned	5147	Locking Bolt for 2″ bbl.	7051	Stock Screw, P.C.
5051	Hammer	5174	Barrel, 4″ (Heavy)	7055	Cylinder Stop Spring
5053	Hand Spring Pin	5357	Cylinder Stop	7056	Stock, P.C., (Left)
5053	Hand Spring Torsion Pin	5395	Frame, round butt, for guns with 2″ barrels, with studs, bushing & lug	7057	Stock, P.C., (Right)
5053	Stirrup Pin			7223	Stock, round butt, (Left)
5053	Trigger Lever Pin			7224	Stock, round butt, (Right)
5054	Sear Spring			7227	Stock Screw for Rd. Butt
5055	Stirrup	5399	Frame, square butt, for guns with 2″ barrels, with studs, bushing & lug	7232	Center Pin for guns with 2″ barrels
5062	Stock Pin				
5064	Strain Screw, square butt				
5071	Thumbpiece Nut				
5072	Trigger				

HANDGUNS

There are basically three kinds of handguns: revolver, semi-automatic, and single-shot.

Revolvers

Revolvers are one of the simplest of all kinds of guns. They utilize a revolving cylinder which holds six, eight, or even occasionally nine cartridges. The cylinder is mated to the barrel and to the firing pin. After the bullet is fired, the cylinder is turned to the next cartridge. There are basically two types of revolvers: single-action and double-action. Single-action revolvers require that you cock the hammer back by hand for each shot. Merely pulling the trigger on the double-action cocks, then fires it.

Revolvers are also made in several different "break-open" types. Solid-frame models have a pin holding the cylinder in place. The pin must be re-

Model 10 Smith & Wesson .38 double-action revolver (above), and exploded view (opposite).

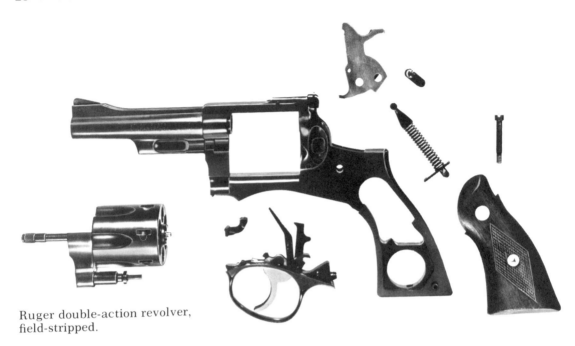

Ruger double-action revolver, field-stripped.

moved for cleaning the cylinder, and sometimes for loading as well. These are the famous Saturday-night specials.

Solid-frame rod-ejector revolvers also have the holding pin for the cylinder. However, these revolvers have a loading-ejection port on the side, often covered by a cover which can be flipped in place. The gun is unloaded by using a spring-loaded rod to push spent shells out the loading ejection port. This is the famous western-style revolver.

Another type of revolver is the solid-frame swing-out. This type has the cylinder located on a swinging or pivoting arm that can be swung out of the frame to allow you to remove spent cartridges and reload the cylinder.

The last type is the top-breaking revolver. This type of revolver is hinged below the cylinder. The cylinder and barrel swing down away from the hammer and grip and breech to allow you to remove or insert cartridges in the cylinder. Most of these are fairly simple guns, and a bit of tinkering, cleaning, and retuning can often result in a pretty workable old gun, unless it is one of the cheap Saturday-night specials.

Semi-Automatic Pistols
Invented by John Browning, these guns require a

Key No.	Part Name
1	Barrel
2	Barrel Bushing
3	Barrel Link
4	Barrel Link Pin
5	Disconnector
6	Ejector
7	Ejector Pin
8	Extractor
9	Firing Pin
10	Firing Pin Spring
11	Firing Pin Stop
12	Front Sight
13	Grip Safety
14	Hammer
15	Hammer Pin
16	Hammer Strut
17	Hammer Strut Pin
18	Magazine Tube Detail Assembly
19	Magazine Catch
20	Magazine Catch Lock
21	Magazine Catch Spring
22	Magazine Follower
23	Magazine Spring
24	Main Spring
25	Main Spring Cap
26	Main Spring Cap Pin
27	Main Spring Housing
28	Main Spring Housing Pin
29	Main Spring Housing Pin Retainer
30	Recoil Spring Plug
31	Plunger Spring
32	Plunger Tube
33	Rear Sight
34	Receiver
35	Recoil Spring
36	Recoil Spring Guide
37	Safety Lock
38	Safety Lock Plunger
39	Sear
40	Sear Pin
41	Sear Spring
42	Slide
43	Slide Stop
44	Slide Stop Plunger
45	Stock—Left Hand
46	Stock—Right Hand
47	Stock Screw (4 Required)
48	Stock Screw Bushing (4 Required)
49	Trigger Assembly

Colt Commander

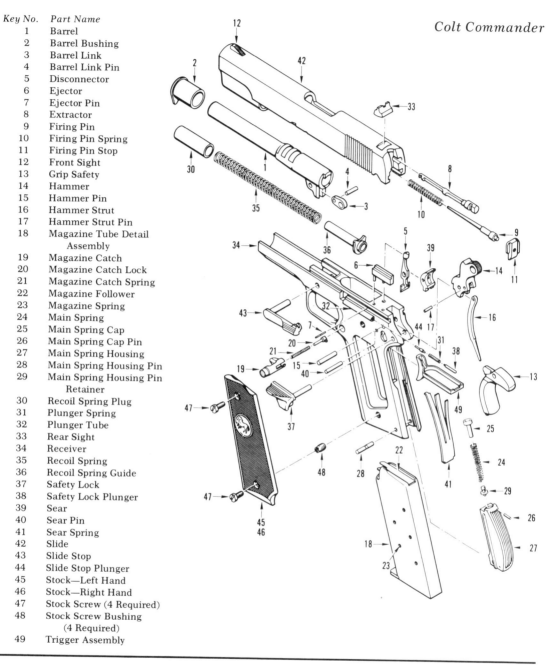

Exploded view of Colt Commander semi-automatic pistol.

trigger pull for each shot. The cartridges in most automatics are carried in a clip which may hold from five to twelve shells. The action in most automatics, especially the lower-caliber guns, is the blowback action described above for automatic rifles. This type of action has no locking system such as a bolt, etc., but utilizes the inertia of the slide

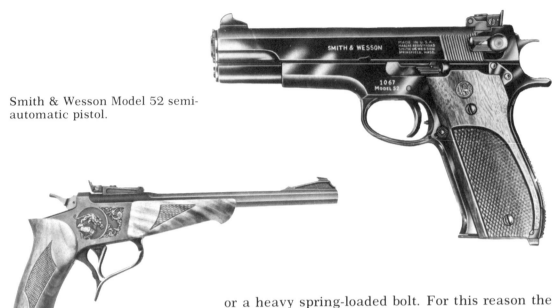

Smith & Wesson Model 52 semi-automatic pistol.

Thompson/Center Contender single-shot pistol.

or a heavy spring-loaded bolt. For this reason the better-made automatics, especially in small caliber, have the barrel fastened to the receiver just like a rifle. The slide with the operating mechanism then extends to the rear of the gun. The larger-caliber pistols, however, utilize a recoil-provided action; too much weight would be needed for the slide and action to operate at heavy larger calibers. In this case the barrel and slide both move toward the rear during firing. Like other automatic guns, autoloading handguns require special care in cleaning and lubricating to make sure there is no rust or dirt buildup.

Single-Shot Handguns

There were many different types of single-shot pistols made. However, there aren't many made today, unless you count the black-powder burners. Most of these used the tip-up type of action, and as a result often became loose and dangerous. One of the newer models being manufactured today is the Contender, which is manufactured by the Thompson/Center Arms Company. Because of their simplicity, these pistols are considered more accurate than either the revolver or the semi-automatic. Other pistols include the Remington bolt-action pistol.

AIR GUNS

Not too many years ago an air gun was merely a step up in a youngster's shooting education. He often got an air gun for use until he could graduate to a rifle or shotgun.

Today, this is still a good practice, but more and more adults are discovering the pleasure and fun of shooting with air guns. Today's air guns are a far cry from the old "Daisy Red Ryder" guns of several years back. One of the reasons for their popularity is that they can be fired in places where powder cartridges can't, and often this means indoors in a basement range if the proper precautions are taken. In addition, the styling of both long guns and pistols now approaches the look and feel of powder guns. The target air guns available are finely honed, fine-shooting arms that any gun lover would enjoy.

Most of the air guns that are made today utilize a compressed-air spring type of action to propel the BB or skirted lead pellet. This normally utilizes a piston on a heavy spring. Cocking the gun compresses the spring. Pressing the trigger releases the spring, which allows it to drive the piston forward with enough power to send the projectile through the small opening. Normally about the only thing that will be needed is a bit of oil through the oil port. A weak spring or a deteriorated leather or rubber washer on top of the piston may also prevent a BB gun from working. Replacing the spring or even just reoiling or replacing the washer will normally do the trick. Just like their big brothers, often air guns are over-oiled, which can cause jamming of parts or deterioration of the washer. Lubricate only in the manner your instruction booklet advises.

The cheaper BB guns normally have a bad trigger pull. This can often be remedied by a bit of judicious filing on the notch engagement or refitting the return springs. However, for safety's sake this shouldn't be overdone on a youngster's first gun. The better models, particularly the CO2 and target-model guns, normally have adjustable trigger pulls. A problem with break-open guns may be a weakened rubber O-ring in the breech which allows air to escape. These can be pulled out and replaced with new ones quite easily.

BLACK-POWDER GUNS

There is a general resurgence of black-powder guns today, as evidenced by the number of new replica guns and kits available on the market.

There are so many different kinds available it isn't possible to describe them here. However, a general statement can be made that guns that are to be shot, as opposed to the "wall hangers," should be kept clean. The worst problem with muzzleloaders is the fouling caused by the black powder. Newer, less fouling powders are being brought out, most notably by the Hodgdon Powder Company.

CHAPTER TWO

SETTING UP A WORKSHOP

Naturally in order to work on guns you'll need a place to do it and the proper tools. Gun work doesn't require as much space as some of the other crafts, such as furniture making. A lot of gun work can often be done on the kitchen table, although a place set aside with a small workbench and storage for tools is much more convenient. If you really like to work with guns and are looking for a place around your home to set up shop, there are a couple of things you should consider: humidity and security.

Let's take humidity first. One of the worst places you can set up a gun shop is in a damp basement. In this type of environment, within a month or so most of your tools, guns, and gun parts will become badly rusted. Ideally the room should be fairly cool and dry.

On the other hand, an unheated garage is also a bad choice. Not only are you limited to the times you can work in it, but security is extremely bad. In most cases the guns you're working on will be torn down. However, you may still have a gun or two standing by waiting for parts, etc., and not only are these guns and even some of the tools dangerous to small children, they're an open invitation to gun thieves. Incidentally, a good way of discouraging gun thieves is to break down a gun and place different parts in different places around the house.

Even a professional gunsmithing shop doesn't have to be large. A gun working bench doesn't have to be elaborate, but it must be solid and have a smooth top.

Actually the best choices for a shop are a dry room in a basement, say near a furnace; a heated, insulated garage (with gun-working room separated and closed off with lock); or a small room in the house.

Although guns look great stacked in racks along the wall, the best storage is in metal or wooden cabinets bolted or fastened to the floor or wall. These cabinets should have heavy-duty doors—not glass—and sturdy locks. You will probably also want to have one such cabinet for storing dangerous equipment or chemicals, such as bluing compounds or other materials that should be kept out of reach of small children.

Stealing firearms has become a favorite activity among thieves and burglars in recent years. The reasons are simple. Guns are easy to dispose of in the underworld—more thugs are getting away with more violent crimes and they need more illegally obtained guns to carry on their business.

There doesn't seem to be any surefire way of stopping the burglar and the sneakthief, but gun owners can do something to raise their chances of getting stolen firearms back. According to a California police official, the recovery rate can increase as much as 40% when a careful record of firearms serial numbers is kept by gun owners. With this information, police can return stolen guns as they turn up. Without serial numbers, recovered guns are destroyed.

And if enough thugs get burned for possessing traceable stolen guns, the criminal might not find firearms so attractive when he goes shopping in other people's homes. Another way of helping to make a gun traceable is to engrave your name on the inside of the gun where it won't be seen readily, using a small hand engraver.

WORKBENCH

A gun-working workbench can be almost anything from a discarded picnic table to an elaborate bench set up exclusively for gunsmithing. One of the most important things I have found in gun-working benches is that they must have a smooth top. An old beat-up wood bench is absolutely useless as a good gun-working bench. The rough top makes it hard to see and handle small gun parts. You can cover a beat-up old top, however, with light-gauge sheet metal, or better yet, tack down a sheet of 1/8-inch hardboard. When it becomes roughened you can merely pull up the hardboard and replace it with a new sheet. A good workbench should have drawers to hold the various specialized gun tools, as well as a rack across the back for those you will be using most often.

The workbench should be of a comfortable height so you can work at it standing up or seated on a tall stool. Most gun work will be done while standing. If you use a stool, one corner of the bench should be shaped so you can get your legs under it while seated on the stool.

LIGHTING

The lighting in the work space is extremely important. There should be plenty of light, and it should be directed straight down on the work area. A fluorescent fixture suspended above the work area, and high enough not to be hit by a gun barrel, is the ideal choice. This provides a good even lighting without any glare from shiny metal parts.

Although not a necessity, a good tool chest can help keep tools lasting longer. You can make your own.

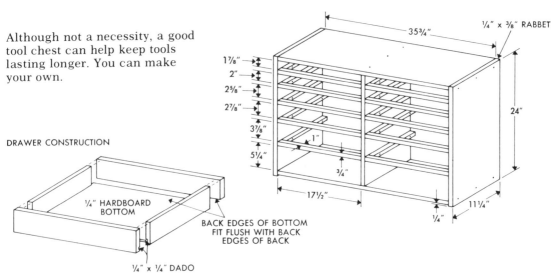

In addition, racks above the workbench can be utilized to hold hand tools.

TOOL STORAGE

A secondhand machinist's chest makes a good place to store tools and parts, although almost anything with drawers or even boxes stored on a shelf will do. If you have the woodworking tools, you can make your own tool chest.

The back of the bench should be fitted with tool holders for such items as punches, chisels, screwdrivers, etc. A pegboard placed above the bench can also be used to hold larger items such as saws, hammers, etc.

VISE

The one thing you must have on your bench is a good swivel machinist's vise. These aren't inexpensive, although you can sometimes pick one up secondhand. This should be securely bolted on one corner end of the workbench so you can use it for vertical as well as horizontal work. These come with serrated steel jaws; for most gun work you will need to pad the jaws. The pads should be made

The main thing you'll need for good gun work is a good solid vise.

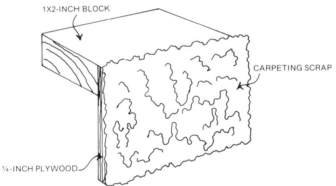

1X2-INCH BLOCK

CARPETING SCRAP

¼-INCH PLYWOOD

These easily made vise pads will protect stocks and receivers.

so you can easily remove them for holding intricate pieces tightly with the metal jaws. Although some craftsmen like to grind the faces off the jaws, this ruins them for holding metal parts securely for jobs such as cutting with a hacksaw.

If you have the space, an excellent method is to fill a 50-gallon drum with concrete and bolt a vise to this. If you do this you can often bolt an anvil on the other side of the barrel and have a sturdy metalworking area.

TOOLS

Gun work is like a lot of other hobbies or skills: You can put as much or little into it as you like. It can be done using nothing more than a good set of screwdrivers and punches, or you can have a shopful of tools, depending on how involved you wish to become.

Part of the fun of gun work is in the tools. Fine tools of all sorts and shapes are a passion with me; my wife says I would rather have a fine set of screwdrivers than the best steak in the world. In any case, regardless of what or how many tools you wish to own, make sure they're of the finest quality. Fine tools will last several lifetimes—I have many handed-down tools from my grandfather and uncle that are as good as the day they were made. On the other hand, a cheap tool is worse than useless. It won't hold an edge, and it is downright dangerous, because you try too hard to get it to work, often causing damage to the gun or yourself.

The variety and number of tools is up to the individual. A great deal of gun work can be done with a good set of screwdrivers, punches, and files as well as the vise and cleaning tools. On the other hand, you can spend a lifetime collecting specialized tools for gun work. Some do a job that just can't be done in any other way. Others are convenient but not essential; you can use basic tools you already have. You can often make up your own tools and jigs. Again, tools are mighty personal, and your selection will depend on what types of guns you have and how involved you get in working on them.

Screwdrivers

The first tools you should acquire are screwdrivers. You just can't get enough screwdrivers for gun work. Probably the most common mistake made by the "gun butcher" is to grab any screwdriver out of the kitchen drawer and attempt to take apart a gun. If the screwdriver doesn't fit the screw head exactly, the result is a torn-up screw head, a screw that is so damaged it can't be removed easily, or worse yet, a burred and scratched receiver or other surrounding metal parts. Anyone who wishes to work on guns should take the time and effort to fit the screwdriver exactly to the screw head.

For most gun work one of the specialized sets of gunsmithing screwdrivers will be the best choice. These have hollow-ground tips and are available in the correct sizes to fit most gun screws. In addition, the better sets come with a ratchet attachment so you can really put pressure on tight and rusty screws. You can also grind screwdrivers to fit the screw head if you have a belt grinder or small bench grinder. If you get a look at a profes-

Special gunsmithing screwdrivers can take a lot of frustration out of gun work.

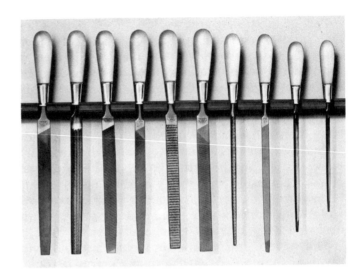

You will need a good assortment of metalworking files, and also rasps for stockwork.

sional gunsmith's bench you'll see literally double handfuls of screwdrivers used for this purpose. Again, however, don't purchase cheap screwdrivers. The soft metal in these won't hold the proper shape under pressure, and the small uncomfortable handles don't provide enough leverage to do the job properly.

Files
Again this can be anything from a couple of files to a double handful. Naturally the more variety of files you have the better. However, in sets of files such as needle files you'll often find the only ones you use are the round and triangular files, so you don't need to purchase full sets. You will need a large mill bastard file in fine cut, a screw-head file, a spring file, and a "knife file." If you plan to do specialized work such as bluing and finishing metal you will need a draw file. You will also need a carding brush for cleaning the files.

Punches
The next tools you'll need are punches. You need a good set of pin punches for driving out pins, as well as a set of roll pin punches, and a small center punch for marking holes to be drilled. Incidentally, a small-size nail set is one of the best types of punches for starting pins in place. The small indented end will not slip off the pin as readily as the flat of a pin punch, and you don't stand as much chance of gouging the surrounding metal with a slip.

Hammers

For most gun work you'll need only three hammers: a small ball-peen or riveting hammer, a rawhide-faced hammer, and a plastic-faced hammer. Don't use an ordinary woodworking hammer for gun work. The face is too hard and may shatter out, causing injury, and in addition the face is flatter so it won't "strike" as well as a metalworking hammer.

Hacksaw

You will also need a hacksaw with a fine blade and an ordinary coarse blade. Purchase only good blades. The hacksaw should be of the high-backed type so you can get in tight places with it without the back rubbing, such as when cutting off bolt handles.

Pliers

Although they are seldom used, a good set of electrician's pliers are sometimes useful. A more useful plier is the lock-jaw type, which can be used when soldering, etc. You will also need flatnose pliers, longnose pliers, roundnose pliers for making small springs, etc., and a pair of side-cutting pliers. Pliers are too frequently misused on guns when a part won't work properly. Many fine guns have been ruined by the improper use of these tools.

Wood Rasps

If you plan to do any stockwork, you will need a variety of wood rasps. Although there are many different kinds and shapes on the market, one of

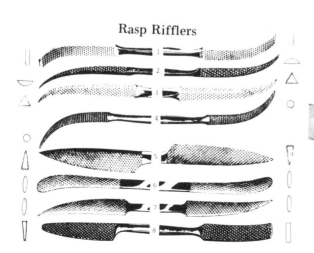

Rasp Rifflers

For tight inletting and final shaping around a pistol grip, you'll need rasps and rifflers in various shapes. The small round and small flat wood rasps shown in the photograph are the ones I use the most.

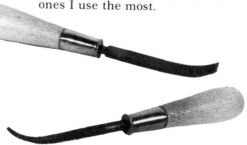

the Stanley Surform tools, along with a standard flat-round cabinet rasp, can be used to do almost any stock shaping. A power rasp that fits in a portable electric drill can't be beat for quick removal of material, but you have to watch it or you can remove too much material. There are also many different kinds of small rasps used by woodworking craftsman that can be used to get in almost any corner or tight space. Of a set I own, however, the only two rasps I have ever used are the small round and the flat. They just can't be beat for some stockwork, particularly on the underside next to the grip where there is just enough rounding and indentation to prevent the use of a standard rasp.

Woodcarving Tools

Along these same lines a good set of woodcarving chisels can make the initial roughing-in of a stock much easier. Again, however, you probably will never use all the chisels in a set. About the only chisels you will need are: straight 18mm gouge, long bent 18mm gouge, straight 2mm parting tool, a straight 10mm patternmaker's chisel, a 10mm patternmaker's gouge, and a set of ordinary woodworking chisels. You will also need a good "Arkansas" stone for honing the chisels, one tapered stone for honing the gouges, and a good wooden mallet for using the chisels. Incidentally if you're into inletting octagon barrels, you can get

You will also need wood chisels, both the ordinary carpenter's chisels and carving gouges in a variety of shapes and sizes.

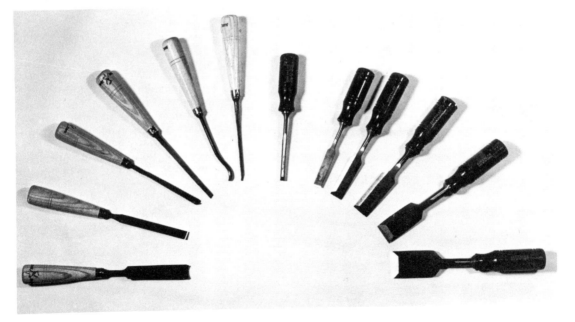

Bottoming Files

Grace Inletting Scrapers

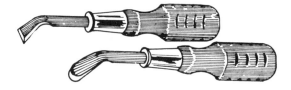

Heavy Barrel Inletting Gouge

Barrel Inletting Rasp

Winton Barrel Inletting Tools

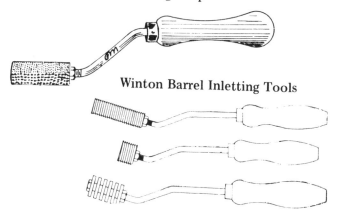

Octagon Barrel Inletting Chisel

Bottoming Chisels

Barrel inletting work such as done on rifle barrels can be done easiest if you have special files, scrapers, and chisels.

a chisel especially for that job, and the handle is offset to allow you to make the flat bottoms and sides.

Inletting Tools

In addition to the regular woodworking tools mentioned above, you will also need other more specialized tools if you plan to do any barrel inletting. Again, you will have to choose according to what particular types of job you intend to do. A good barrel-inletting rasp can be used to do most of the

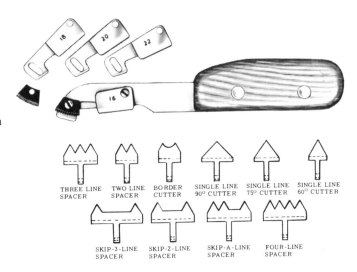

THREE LINE SPACER TWO LINE SPACER BORDER CUTTER SINGLE LINE 90° CUTTER SINGLE LINE 75° CUTTER SINGLE LINE 60° CUTTER

SKIP-3-LINE SPACER SKIP-2-LINE SPACER SKIP-A-LINE SPACER FOUR-LINE SPACER

One of the most fascinating woodworking projects for the gun worker is checkering. For this you'll need a set of checkering tools.

One forgotten old-time craftsman's tool is the scraper. This will put a finish on a gunstock that all the sanding in the world won't accomplish. It is available in a variety of shapes.

rough work, then final shaping can be done with a barrel-inletting tool, which is a sort of multicutter scraper that can be pulled along the bottom of the barrel groove. Bottoming files are also specialized tools used for this work and are essential for final cutting in small areas such as around a shotgun lock or rifle action.

Checkering Tools

One of the most interesting and fascinating jobs in gun work is checkering. The best bet is to purchase a checkering kit, although you can get by with a small veining tool, a single-line cutter, and a double-line cutter. For the first-time checkering get a set with no more than 189 lines per inch. A checkering cradle can also be a great help. You can easily make your own.

If you wish to try your hand at stockmaking you might do well to purchase a complete stockmaking set, which consists of the rasps, chisels, checkering tools, and special inletting tools needed for the job.

More Vises

In addition to the large vise you will need a small pin vise for handling small screws, as well as a drill-press vise if you intend to do any extensive metalwork. A set of small parallel-jaw metal clamps can be used for such chores as holding sights in place for soldering, etc.

You will also need a hollow pin vise.

Measuring Tools

Most measuring jobs can be handled with a vernier caliper, which takes both inside and outside measurements. A small measuring tape is also handy for rough measurements of stocks, etc.

Taps and Dies

A good set of taps and dies is extremely important to quality gun work. Although a standard set sold through most hardware stores can be used, a special set made up just for gunsmithing is the best choice. Regardless of what the set is, make sure you have a couple of 6×48 taps in a carbon or high-speed steel. If you plan on working on hardened-steel receivers such as the Enfield, a tap-holding jig made by B-Square Co. which fits in your drill press can be a great help. In use, the hole is drilled using the drill press, the jig fits into the drill press collet, and the tap is automatically aligned properly with the hole. In addition, tap extractors and screw extractors can save many a headache and problem.

POWER TOOLS

Hand Grinder

There are a few power tools that are essential for gunwork other than cleaning, etc. The most important is a small bench grinder. This can be used to regrind tool faces and edges, to make small parts, and, if fitted with a wire wheel, to polish metal. In addition, cloth wheels can also be fitted to the grinder spindle and when used with abrasive sticks can be used for metal polishing, such as when replating.

Portable Electric Drill

The next power tool is a portable electric drill. It can be used for many jobs, including polishing bores as shown in Chapter 5. It should not be used for metal-drilling jobs unless the drill can be held in a drill-press jig and the metal clamped to the press table for precision drilling.

Drill Press

In fact, a drill press is almost essential for very extensive gun work. The extreme precision of most drilling jobs requires a method of ensuring that the hole is drilled to proper depth, at the right angle, etc. Incidentally, this is one of the larger power tools that can often be found in garage sales. Many times when fitted with a new motor it can be made as good as new. Make sure, however, there is no play in the head and that the press can be locked perfectly true with the press table to ensure properly bored holes. The drill press should be a variable-speed so you can bore holes in hardened steel with the slow speeds and do wood-boring jobs with a faster speed.

Belt Grinder

Although not a necessity, a belt grinder is one of the handiest tools you can own. The belt can be used to sharpen tools, and it doesn't heat up the metal as much as a wheel grinder does, so you don't take as much risk of ruining a fine tool. In addition, it can be used to grind small parts quite easily. The large flat table on front of the grinder makes it easy to hold parts with a pair of lock-joint

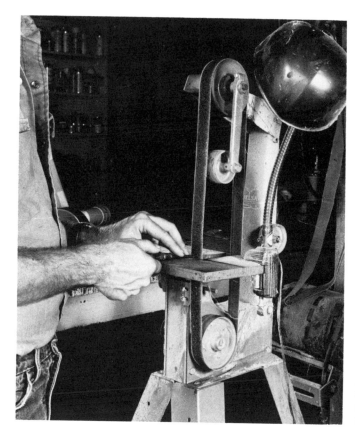

A belt grinder can be used to sharpen tools or to cut wood or metal, depending on the belt used.

pliers or a small clamp. When fitted with a coarse belt the belt grinder will do a great job of rough-shaping wood, if you keep the wood moving so the narrow belt doesn't cut too fast in one spot.

Hand Grinder

You will also need a small hand grinder, such as the Dremel Moto-Tool, with accessories. This just can't be beat for fast shaping of inletted areas, grinding and polishing small metal parts, and with a little practice, even wood engraving. A small metal-engraving tool can also be used to engrave your name on the inside of gun parts for later identification.

Torch

A propane or gas torch can be used for everything from soldering to heat-treating or bluing small parts such as screws.

Welder

Although there is little welding done in most home gun work, there is quite a bit of brazing as well as silver soldering, and a small welding-torch kit can be a great help. These small units are handy enough for the small welding jobs needed, such as welding on bolt handles or brazing pieces back together.

Drill Bits

You will need an assortment of drill bits, and a set of bits can be mighty expensive when you don't use but a half-dozen or so. Purchase only those that you need in quality bits, adding to your set as you need them. You will also need a drill-bit gauge and a screw-thread gauge.

Safety Goggles

A pair of safety goggles, or, better yet, a full face shield, is a must when grinding and polishing metal.

SPECIALIZED TOOLS

In addition to the standard tools listed, there are an infinite number of specialized tools that gunsmiths have designed over the years to help do a job better, or even those that are a must for certain jobs. There is no need to purchase these tools until you have a specific need for them.

Barrel Sight Drill Jig

A V-block guide which is used to bore precision holes in rifle and barrels and shotgun ramps for installing front bead sights.

Shotgun Sight Installer

A small gripping tool that enables you to quickly and easily install a bead sight on a gun without damaging the surrounding metal.

Rib Sight Jig

There are a number of these small jigs that can be used to locate and bore the holes in a rib on a single- or double-barrel shotgun.

In addition to the regular tools, there are a great number of specialized gun working tools. If you plan on doing much gun work, you'll appreciate the help they give on certain jobs. It's a good idea to purchase these a few at a time as you need them.

Guard-Screw Wrenches and Pins

When inletting bolt actions you'll do a lot of assembling and disassembling to fit the action properly in place. These are quicker than using the guard screws from the action and prevent tearing up the guard screws with constant use during the fitting.

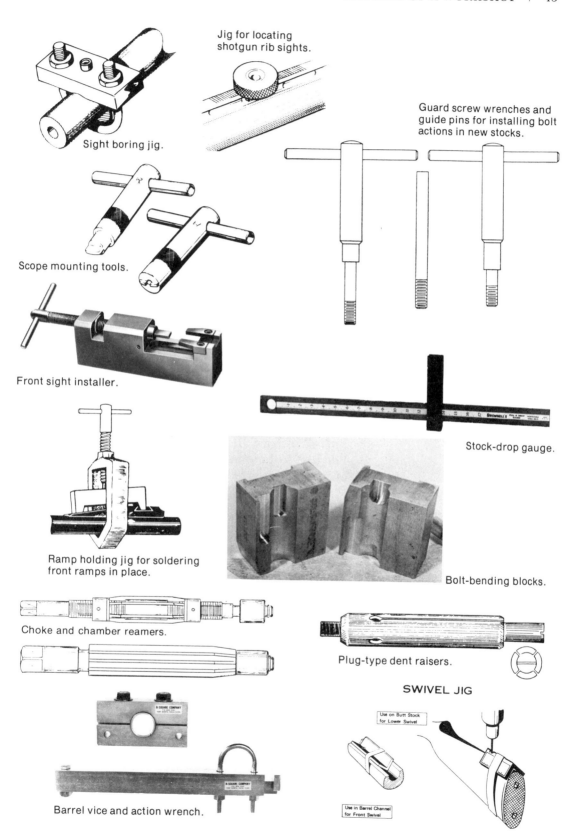

Sight boring jig.

Jig for locating shotgun rib sights.

Guard screw wrenches and guide pins for installing bolt actions in new stocks.

Scope mounting tools.

Front sight installer.

Stock-drop gauge.

Ramp holding jig for soldering front ramps in place.

Bolt-bending blocks.

Choke and chamber reamers.

Plug-type dent raisers.

SWIVEL JIG

Barrel vice and action wrench.

Use on Butt Stock for Lower Swivel

Use in Barrel Channel for Front Swivel

Scope-Mounting Tools

If you plan to do very much scope-mounting work, a scope-mounting tool for the various scopes will prevent burring and marring of the screws and provide more leverage than a large screwdriver.

Front-Sight Pusher

Although front sights can be removed and installed using a small pin punch and hammer, these jigs do the job easier and prevent marring the surrounding metal.

Ramp-Soldering Jig

Another handy tool that can be used instead of a pair of parallel-jaw clamps.

Stock-Drop Gauges

When fitting a shotgun stock to the proper length to suit, a gunstock gauge can be more accurate than the old methods of measuring such as with a carpenter's square. Shown is the Brownell pull and drop gauge, which measures the stock pull and the drop at the heel.

Bolt-Bending Blocks

For use in bending bolt handles on bolts such as Mauser, Springfield, and Japanese rifles.

Barrel Vise and Action Wrench

When removing a barrel from the action, something must be used to firmly clamp the barrel and action while turning the barrel. These two tools make the hard job much easier.

Shotgun Choke Gauges and Reamers

An excellent shotgun choking set is available from Brownell's; it includes reamers, barrel calipers, and a barrel hone. For true choke work you should also have chamber reamers. These should be used first, then the gun patterned, and follow with the choke alteration as desired.

Hydraulic Dent Raiser

A tool that won't get much use but can't be substituted for when you need it. It is used much in the same manner as removing a dent from an automobile body.

Bore Light
A small penlight tool that enables you to see into small tight places such as actions, bores, etc.

Belt and Disc Sander
The best method of installing a recoil pad is to use a disc sander to cut down the recoil pad at the same time you cut down the stock, or if on a finished stock to fit the outline of the finished stock.

Swivel Jig and Drill Set
The better ones can be used to guide the bit on the gun stock, then can be turned upside down to go into the barrel channel to bore the front swivel hole. The drill set has a locking collar that stops bits at the correct depth.

Snap Caps
A set of snap caps in each gauge or to fit each of your guns will prevent visitors from ruining firing pins.

Tweezers
A lot of gun work involves tiny detailed pieces, and several shop tweezers can be a great help. Incidentally, if you can get a doctor friend to get you some, medical tweezers are a much better choice than the kinds sold for shop work. They'll last longer and provide better gripping power.

Metal-Engraving Tools
This is one area you may want to think about for some time before tackling. Metal engraving is a highly specialized craft that takes a lot of time and practice. However, in today's market for fine guns you can often more than pay for your time once you learn the skills. The tools needed for the job are quite expensive and highly specialized, so you might wish to get a book on the subject before you begin to think about this portion of gun work.

Other Special Tools
There are many tools in addition to those mentioned before that are made for specific guns, such as a bushing wrench used to remove or reseat bushings on Colt .45 guns, or Mauser pliers used to place the collar on the bolt of a Mauser, or a Smith & Wesson crane-alignment tool.

CHAPTER THREE

CLEANING GUNS

Proper cleaning of a gun can not only extend its lifetime and improve its appearance, but can also help maintain its accuracy and make it safer. Some guns may need more frequent cleaning than others, depending on the climate they're used in, how frequently they're used, and even what type of ammunition is fired through them. Although most of the modern ammunition used today doesn't cause many problems, some high-velocity ammunition can cause barrel fouling. Guns using this type of ammunition should be cleaned more often and more thoroughly.

All guns should be periodically cleaned, both in the field and during, after, and before the season. Guns that are fired quite frequently, such as target guns, should be cleaned at least after every fifty rounds. Before the season starts, clean the gun thoroughly to remove all dust and even the occasional "mud dauber nest" that finds its way into the barrel. During the season a light cleaning will suffice unless the gun has seen wet or heavy action. Then it should receive a thorough cleaning. After the season is over, go over the entire gun, dismantling it as much as is possible and cleaning away all oil and dirt, then oiling and lubricating again for storage.

Breech-opening guns may be easily cleaned and inspected by opening at the breech. When cleaning revolvers, make sure you get chamber and cylinder

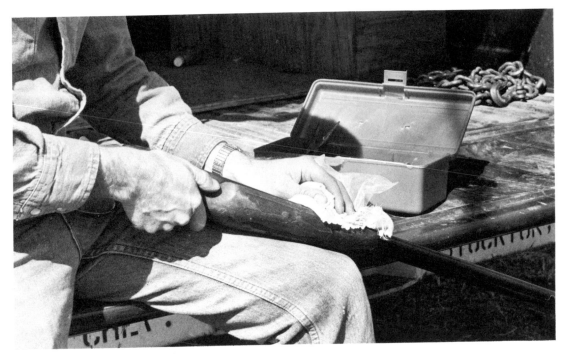

Proper gun care begins in the field. I carry a small cleaning kit in my truck. A soft cloth well saturated with gun oil and stored in a plastic bag is handy to wipe guns down after hunting.

ratchet clean as well as the breech face on .22 automatics. Debris here keeps the extractor too far out to work properly. Bolt-action rifles and shotguns can be cleaned easily by using a cleaning guide made of a drilled-out dowel fitted into the chamber after the bolt is removed. This prevents damaging the opening end of the chamber with the cleaning equipment. Pump, lever, and automatic guns are the hardest to clean because they can't be disassembled as easily for cleaning.

CLEANING IN THE FIELD

Cleaning and caring for guns starts in the field. If you throw a wet, fouled gun into a tight gun case in the back of a station wagon and drive a couple of hundred miles back home from a hunting trip, by the time you get home, rust can already be starting to form on the gun. Once rust starts to form it is almost impossible to stop. One solution is to keep a small gun-care kit in your automobile. After shooting, give your gun a light going over so it will be protected until you can get it home for a more thorough cleaning. The kit should consist of a small plastic tackle box, a soft cloth well wetted with gun oil (this is kept in an airtight plastic bag), a can of rust-preventive oil (WD-40), a pair of

A light dust spraying with a rust preventive will help keep rust from starting before the gun can be cleaned properly.

pliers, a small screwdriver, a small cleaning rod or a piece of piano wire, and patches, should the barrel need to be cleaned of dirt.

Normally the most that needs to be done is to wipe down the outside of the gun with a dry cloth, then follow with a cloth and gun oil. Open the gun action and give a light dusting coat with the rust preventive. Set the gun aside for a moment and allow any excess oil to run out, then place the gun in the case. The screwdriver is used for small emergency repairs. I once lost a screw out of a trigger guard on a favorite double during a quail hunt only because I didn't have anything with me to tighten it with.

One of the most common mishaps in the field is stumbling and sticking the end of a gun barrel in the snow, mud, or dirt. Unless this is cleaned out, the gun can explode, ruining not only the gun, but the gunner as well. The first step is to *unload the gun*, and then, holding the muzzle down, use a sharp object such as a stick or pocketknife blade to remove the obstruction. Be careful not to nick the end of the barrel. Blow through the barrel to remove any of the loose debris, blowing from the breech end. If possible, hold the gun up to the light and examine the barrel to make sure all the debris is out. You may wish to take the gun back to your

The first step in clearing a fouled muzzle is to *unload gun*, then turn the muzzle down and use a sharp object to remove the mud, snow, etc. Be careful not to nick the inside of the muzzle. Then blow out the remainder of the debris and inspect by looking through the barrel if possible.

auto or camp and fish the piano wire through the barrel. Then pull a patch soaked in oil through the barrel to remove any material that may still be left in the barrel.

When transporting a gun, make sure you keep it well protected. Don't just throw it in the back with your other gear. Although a gun rack on a truck or station wagon looks impressive it is also an invitation to sticky-fingered people. Instead, store the gun in a rack behind the seat, or on the floorboards and placed in a good case. If the day is clear and dry, put the gun in the case, zip it up, and place in the rack. If the day has been wet and nasty, put the gun in the case, but don't close it up. Even with the protective oil and spray of rust preventive you may not reach all the tight spots and rust can start if the gun is enclosed in such a manner that moisture cannot escape.

CLEANING AT HOME

Regardless of what type of cleaning you do in the field, once you're home your guns should be thoroughly cleaned, relubricated, and stored in a dry, safe place. The amount of cleaning can vary from the light going-over after a dove hunt to a complete cleaning and reoiling after a soggy day of goose hunting. In addition to this regular type of cleaning, guns may also occasionally require a complete dismantling and cleaning. Some guns are easily taken apart by most gun owners. Other guns, such as lever-action rifles, should be taken to a professional gunsmith for complete dismantling and a thorough cleaning.

Clean all guns horizontally, except automatic handguns, which should be cleaned upside down.

CLEANING TOOLS

You can purchase a simple cleaning kit which will contain most of the items you will need for cleaning your guns. However, if you have a variety of guns, you will need some specialized tools for cleaning them properly. The kits normally contain cleaning solvents, gun oil, patches, cleaning tray, a rod, and a cleaning brush. Make sure you purchase a kit with the proper-size tools to fit your caliber or gauge gun. If you're purchasing cleaning tools separately, the first thing you will need is a cleaning rod. There are several different types: jointed aluminum or wood, which are good for

You can purchase a full kit for cleaning your gun, or purchase the separate materials and tools needed specifically for your gun or guns.

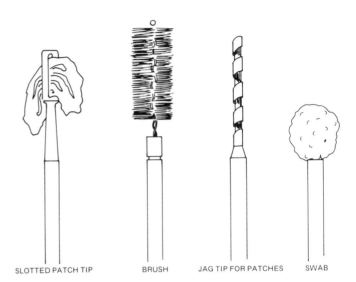

The four types of cleaning tips.

SLOTTED PATCH TIP   BRUSH   JAG TIP FOR PATCHES   SWAB

shotguns, and solid steel rods for use in cleaning rifles. Don't use a jointed aluminum rod for cleaning a rifle, as it isn't strong enough and may bend from the pressure needed to force the proper-size cleaning brushes through the barrel. There are several different types of cleaning-rod tips available; the most popular are shown here. Most of these can be screwed into a hollow aluminum, wooden, or steel cleaning rod. The first shown is a slotted patch which is used for pushing cleaning patches through the barrel. The second shown is a cleaning brush. These may be bronze or brass. The third type shown is a jag tip, which is also used with cleaning patches. The last type shown is a wool swab. The swabs, brushes, and patches should be purchased in the proper size for the caliber or gauge of your shotgun, rifle, or handgun. You will also need wool mops or swabs sized to fit your gun, as well as wire-bristle chamber-cleaning brushes. These can merely be the next-larger-size brush for cleaning shotguns.

Patches can be either purchased or cut from old diapers or flannel shirts. You will also need powder-cleaning solvent and rust-preventive oil such as WD-40, gun oil, swabs, and gun grease. Gun grease should be a white gun lubricant containing molybdenum disulfide.

CLEANING STEPS

A gun can be cleaned almost anywhere, but it's a good idea to have a soft cloth to lay the parts on,

The barrels from a double-barrel shotgun are shown removed from the gun and clamped in the vise for easier, more thorough cleaning.

and also one that has a bit of nap to prevent small parts from rolling around and getting lost. Normally you won't have to dismantle a gun completely for cleaning, but partially breaking it down will help you get to all those old weed seeds, dirt, oil, and grease. The best method of cleaning a rifle or a shotgun is to place it in a well-padded vise, leaving both hands free to operate the cleaning rod. This not only provides a good way of getting a better cleaning job, but by using the rod in this manner you will avoid nicking or damaging the ends of the barrel with the cleaning rod. In some cases, removing the barrel may make cleaning easier. The steps in cleaning a barrel are quite simple and it pays to follow them in order.

1. The first step is to place gun-cleaning solvent on a wool mop or swab and run it through the barrel several times. When cleaning rifled guns, if possible push the brush, patch, etc. through from the breech toward the muzzle. Unscrew the tip, pull the rod back through, fasten the tip back in place, and repeat. If you pull the tip back through the barrel you stand a chance of ruining the rifling at the crown of the muzzle. Naturally on lever-actions you have to go from the muzzle toward the breech.

2. The second step is to fit a bristle brush to the end of the cleaning rod and force it through several times to loosen the fouling in the barrel. Use only a brush of the proper size to fit your particular gun.

3. The third step is to clean the chamber. Most of us are pretty particular about the bore of our guns, but often neglect the chamber. A clean chamber is just as important as a clean bore. If

Step 1: A swab is saturated with nitro-powder cleaning solution and run through the barrel several times.

Step 2: Then a brass bristle brush of the proper size is used to remove as much of the fouling and powder residue as possible. Normally one or two passes will suffice. The brush can be removed from the cleaning rod and swirled around the end of the barrel to remove any residue clinging to the muzzle.

Step 3: Use the next-larger size brush to clean out the chambers.

Step 4: Use cloth patches to remove all the debris that has been loosened, using successive patches until they come out clean, then saturate patch with gun oil and run it through the barrel several times.

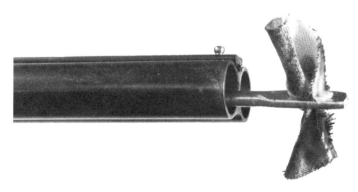

a gun has misfire, jamming, or extraction problems, the chamber may be rough, rusted, or loaded up with wax or crud from plastic shells. Each time you clean your gun, inspect and clean the chamber as well. Breech-opening shotguns can easily be cleaned using the next-larger-size cleaning brush, or you can purchase special chamber-cleaning brushes. Some of these are made so the handles can be bent, allowing you to clean automatic or pump-action shotguns. You can also use steel wool on a brush for light polishing. There are also chamber-cleaning tools for some rifle calibers. However, you can easily make up your own chamber-cleaning tools for either rifles or shotguns. Merely make up a mandrel of $3/16$-inch cold-rolled steel rod. Slot the end with a fine-toothed hacksaw. Place a bit of crocus cloth in the slot and turn the cleaning tool around inside the chamber with your fingers to cut away the rust. Spraying in a bit of WD-40 first will help. To make up the same type of chamber-polishing tool for shotguns, put a drilled dowel over the steel rod, then cut a slot in it for the crocus cloth. In effect you're lapping the chamber, but this should not be confused with the lapping done by professional gunsmiths to "reshape" a chamber. Only a very light bit of polishing is needed. If the chamber is in too bad shape, take the gun to a gunsmith and have him lap and polish or reshape the chamber.

4. The fourth step is to saturate a patch with cleaning solvent and run it through the gun several times. Then remove the dirty patch and use a clean dry patch to remove as much solvent as possible. Place a bit of gun oil on a new patch and run it through the barrel several times to make sure the barrel is well oiled and protected.

5. The fifth step is to sight through the barrel toward light to see if any dirt has been missed.

FOULING AND RUSTING

Although a badly rusted barrel may cause more trouble than the average gun owner wants to tackle, one that is slightly rusted or somewhat fouled with lead can be cleaned in one of two methods. For a shotgun, make up a jig as shown in the illustration. Cut the handle end off a steel cleaning rod so it can be chucked in a portable electric drill. Wrap 4/0 steel wool around a proper-size cleaning

STEEL WOOL OR CLEANING BRUSH

BRUSH WELDED TO ¼-INCH STEEL ROD OR PLACED ON STEEL CLEANING ROD

To get a shotgun barrel free of lead deposits, use a cleaning jig in a portable electric drill.

brush. Chuck the modified cleaning tool in a portable electric drill and use this to clean away lead deposits.

If the bore of a rifle or handgun is badly fouled you can often clean it with a bore solvent (DU-OL) or an ammonia solution. Use solution made up of:

6 oz. strong ammonia
1 oz. ammonium persulphate
200 grains ammonium carbonate
4 oz. rainwater or distilled water

Use ammonia purchased from a drugstore, not the regular household kind. Place a cork in the breech, stand the gun up, and use a small funnel to pour the solution in the muzzle. Allow to stand for 30 to 40 minutes, then pour out, being careful not to get any on the outside of the barrel or especially on the wood portions. Run several patches soaked in hot water through the barrel. Then use a hair dryer on hot to quickly dry the barrel.

Another method of cleaning is to pour boiling water through the barrel. Again dry, then oil with patches. You can also remove leading by boiling the gun in water. If you wish to disassemble a gun such as a hand gun entirely, you can boil the parts in hot water to which a bit of dish detergent has been added. Then boil in clean water and remove with tongs. The metal will dry immediately from the heat. On many handguns, all you need to do is remove the grips, then drop the gun in boiling water. When the gun is removed it will flash-dry quickly enough to stop rusting.

Gun parts can also be cleaned by soaking in lacquer thinner for an hour or two. But remember—lacquer thinner is extremely flammable. Then remove, allow to dry, wipe off the white residue left by the cleaner or use a hair dryer to hasten drying, and reoil. Squirt a bit of oil in place with a needle oiler and use a hair dryer on cool to force the oil into the works.

When the bore and mechanism are clean, wipe

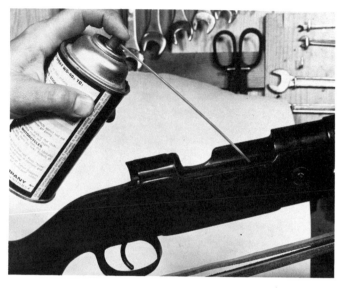

Use a needle oiler for those hard-to-reach spots.

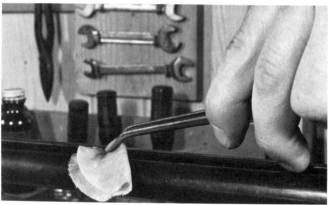

Small, hard-to-get-to areas can be cleaned and oiled with a pair of tweezers and a barrel-cleaning patch soaked in oil.

the exterior of the barrel and all other metal with a cloth saturated with a good rust-preventive gun oil such as Brownell's. Areas such as around hammers on rifles and handguns and the under portion of ribs on shotguns can be cleaned and oiled using patches and tweezers.

A tiny speck of rust can often be removed by spraying a bit of WD-40 on it, allowing it to set for about an hour, then using extremely fine steel wool to buff down the rust. Deeply pitted rust should be treated differently, as explained in Chapter 5. Then again give a light dust coating of rust-preventive oil. A small hand grinder fitted with a tiny steel-wool brush can also be used to burnish the metal parts of the gun and remove rust spots, but be careful not to hold the brush in one spot too long or it will eat away the bluing or metal finish.

Once the metal parts are clean, go over the

Metal surfaces can be polished with a small hand grinder and polishing wheel, but be careful not to cut too deeply into metal.

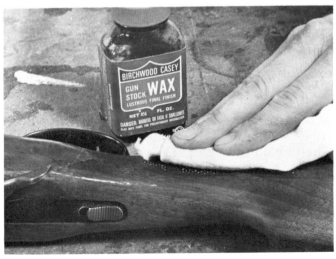

Wash mud and dirt off the stock, using a bit of dish detergent in water, then rinse off the soapy water and apply a coat of gunstock wax. Allow to dry and buff to soft sheen.

Don't forget to clean the lenses on rifle scopes using a fine cloth and alcohol, or better yet, camera-lens cleaning tissues.

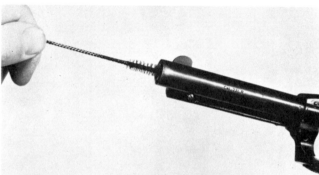

If possible, it's best to disassemble handguns before cleaning. Make sure the cylinder is thoroughly cleaned. A small brass-bristle brush makes short work of cleaning the ratchet on the cylinder.

Store cleaned and oiled guns upside down so the excess oil can run out of them instead of collecting in the insides, gumming up, and soaking the wood.

stock, fore-end, etc. with a damp cloth dipped in water with a bit of dish washing detergent added. Then wipe clean with clear water and allow to dry thoroughly. Apply a bit of gunstock wax to the stock and buff it down thoroughly, or if the stock is oil-finished, use a bit of linseed oil on a soft cloth to buff it down. Reassemble the gun and wipe it down thoroughly with a cloth dipped in a rust-preventive oil and remove all fingerprints, etc. that might cause the metal to rust while the gun is not in use.

Stand the gun up, *muzzle down*, for about a day and allow all excess oil to run out the muzzle. I have replaced more than one shotgun stock for people who have allowed oiled guns to sit in the standard way, allowing oil to soak into the stock, where it will eventually weaken the wood.

CLEANING MUZZLELOADERS

Muzzleloaders have problems all their own. Black-powder burners must be completely cleaned or moisture is drawn by the black-powder residue, which results in corrosion and a ruined gun.

After shooting and while still in the field, run a patch moistened with rust-preventive oil down the barrel, then dust-spray lock, nipple, hammer, etc.

When you get home, take off the nipple and use a brush and powder solvent to remove the powder residue from the barrel. Run dry cleaning patches through the bore, then run a spit patch, or one dipped in water and wrung out, through the barrel to remove the powder residue. Follow with dry patches to remove water. Turn the barrel upside down for a few minutes, then reoil the bore with rust-preventive oil.

For an especially good cleaning job, disassemble the gun and pour boiling water through it or boil small parts in a pan and reoil.

If you plan to store the gun for some time, use the hot-water treatment, then use a heavy gun grease such as Rig for coating the metal. Before you use the gun again this grease must be thoroughly cleaned out.

Cleaning muzzleloaders is another thing entirely. A patch dampened with water should occasionally be run down the barrel while still in the field. Then after the day's shooting, clean with special cleaners used for muzzleloaders, or remove barrel, take out nipple, and pour boiling water through the barrel. Then swab with gun oil and reassemble.

CHAPTER FOUR

REPAIRING, ALTERING, AND MAKING GUNSTOCKS

Next to cleaning, refinishing a gunstock is one of the most popular home gun projects. Like all gun work, the results are often quite different depending on the person doing the job. The appearance of many a fine gun has literally been destroyed by a poorly refinished stock. And it's a shame, because the job is easy, even for the first-timer if he uses good-quality materials and takes the time to use them properly.

The most common mistake is applying a finish with a brush. No amount of sanding or polishing will change this type of finish into a good professional-looking job. The old-time gunstocks had a hand-rubbed oil finish, and many of the better stocks today have an oil-based finish. These not only will withstand the weather better, but they won't chip and peel as will some of the more "standard" finishes used for other woodworking projects. Birchwood Casey makes a very fine oil finish that can be applied by aerosol can, but for the purists, there are also many fine oil-based finishes that can be applied by hand. The new oil-based finishes don't require as much time or skill as the old-fashioned linseed-oil finishes, yet they provide a good even finish.

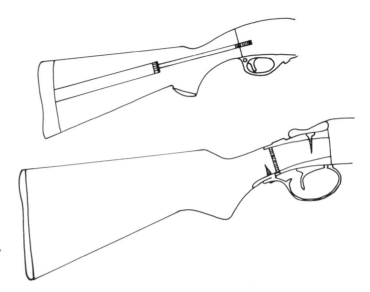

The stock may be held in place by a single stock bolt, or by several screws.

STOCK REMOVAL

In many cases the hardest part of stockwork is removing the old stock. Each and every gun seems to present its own problems.

Most pump and auto shotguns are held together by a bolt through the stock from the rear. Removing the recoil pad gives access to this bolt. The bolt may be screw-slotted, hex-head, or both. Make sure you have a good solid heavy-duty screwdriver or socket wrench with an extension to remove this, and make sure the tool fits the bolt properly. If you tear up an old bolt, you'll have to literally destroy the stock to remove it, and this is normally an unnecessary chore.

Double-barrel shotguns are fairly simple to remove stocks from. However, there are several screws holding them together, so if you're sure you've got them all but the stock won't pull off or out, look again. Some may also have stock bolts.

Stocks from bolt-action rifles are the easiest to remove. If you aren't familiar with the gun, get a copy of the parts sheet from the manufacturer if you can.

Use a small metal cookie sheet or plastic dish to keep all of the gun parts in. Keep the screws in a smaller container such as a jar or can. If you're not sure of yourself, make a rough sketch of how the gun comes apart as you disassemble it. In some cases you must be sure to get the proper-length screw in each hole when reassembling the gun.

After removing the stock from the gun, remove all pieces from the stock—the recoil pad, grip caps, etc. In some cases these may be glued on, so use a sharp knife or chisel to carefully loosen them.

Recoil pads are held in place with concealed screws through the back. Use a narrow-blade screwdriver and look for the tiny X-cuts in the back of the pad. Push the screwdriver through these and wiggle it until you find the screw slot, then carefully remove the screw. Make sure you hold the blade tightly in the slot. If you tear up the slot you will probably destroy the pad in getting it off.

REFINISHING STOCKS

Cover a table or work surface with several layers of newspaper and lay the gun down on this. Coat the entire surface of the stock with a good paint-and-varnish stripper—the kind that can be rinsed off with water. Allow the stripper to work until the old finish is bubbled up all over. If there are dry places on the stock, or places where the finish hasn't been loosened, paint on more stripper (over the entire stock to keep previously loosened paint from drying out) and allow it to work a bit longer. The secret in easy stripping is to allow the stripper to do the work for you. But you must keep the surface wet with stripper. If it's allowed to dry out, it becomes quite a bit harder to work with, and if you're using a cheap stripper you may even "set"

In this case the old stock is being stripped of all old finish. Ordinary paint stripper is painted on and allowed to bubble thoroughly, then washed off using wet steel wool. Follow with thorough washing in alcohol or lacquer thinner. Then wipe down with tack cloth.

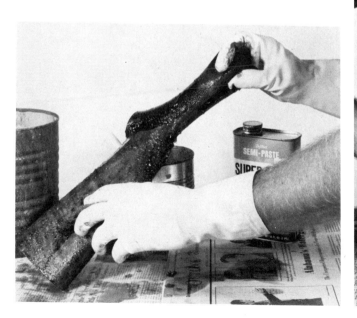

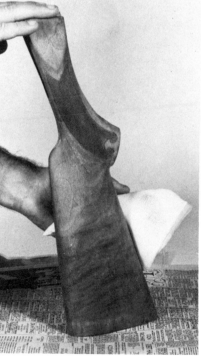

the finish. Then it becomes almost impossible to remove.

When all finish has bubbled loose, use a medium-grit steel wool, dipped in water, to scrub away all loosened finish, stripper, stain, etc. Wear rubber gloves to protect your hands. Make sure you get down in all tight areas, especially the checkering. Flush the stock thoroughly with a hose or faucet to wash all debris away. Then allow it to dry thoroughly. Wash a second time, using lacquer thinner to remove all tiny bits of finish, dust, and oils, then allow to dry.

Refilling and Restaining
In most cases, if the stock is a good-quality stock, you won't need to refill it or even restain it. The

There are many different types of stock finishes that can be used. If you prefer a spray finish, make a spray booth with a small cardboard box and coathanger wire. If you prefer a more traditional finish, use a wipe-on oil finish.

hard, tight-grained wood used in better-quality stocks will retain these materials. If you do need to refill or restain the stock, do so at this time. A paste wood filler can be applied, mixed in with a nonpenetrating oil stain, or the two can be applied separately. Don't overdo the staining on a gunstock. Even if the wood grain isn't the best, it will look better natural than it will with a heavy coat of stain. Apply stain and/or filler materials according to directions on the can and allow to dry overnight. From this point on, refinishing the gunstock is the same whether you have applied the stain and/or filler or not.

Applying the New Finish

Before applying the finish, wipe down the entire stock with a tack cloth, to remove all dirt, oil, and dust. After this, try to handle the stock by the ends to keep fingerprints off the unfinished wood.

There are many different gunstock finishes available. The better ones are oil-based. One of the easiest and best finishes is an oil finish in an aerosol can. However, the same finish is available in a rub-on solution for the purists. In either case, the secret to a good gunstock finish, one that will withstand abuse and weathering, is to apply many light coats of finish, sanding between each to produce the desired covering and sheen. Above all, don't paint the finish on with a brush. This is a common mistake that has ruined many a fine gunstock. Nothing looks worse than a glossy gunstock. It should have depth and transparency so the grain will show through, yet have adequate protection for the wood and have the look of a hand-rubbed satiny-smooth sheen.

To achieve the desired covering you may have to apply from six to ten coats of finish, using a soft cloth, or better yet, your fingertips. After all but the last couple of coats, use 400-grit open-coat finishing paper to smooth down the finish. Be careful on the checkering or any carving; you don't want to knock the finish off the high spots. Some gun finishers like to use a felt pad between sanding paper and hand to even it out and prevent the chance of a sharp edge of paper cutting into the finish too much in one spot. Use a fine-bristle brass brush to clean the sanding dust and finish out of the checkering and carved portions of the stock.

Use 4/0 or extra-fine steel wool to rub down the stock after the next-to-last two coats. Then use

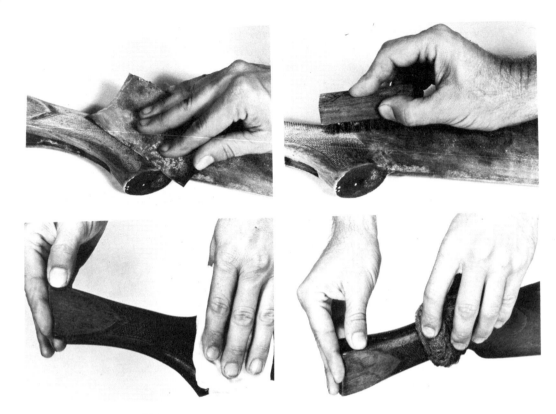

The first few coats should be sanded smooth utilizing 240-grit wet-or-dry paper. Use a small brass bristle brush to clean debris out of checkering, then rub with tack cloth and apply next coat of finish. The last few coats of finish are rubbed down with 4/0 steel wool.

stock rubbing compound and a soft cloth or paste floor wax and extra-fine steel wool to rub the stock down after the last coat. Be extra-careful on this to keep from knocking the finish from the high spots of gun and to keep an evenness to the finish. If done properly, this will cut the garish look of the finish down to a satin sheen, not a dull look. Then apply a good coat of gunstock polish to the stock to bring out the sheen and satiny texture.

Put the recoil pad and other fixtures back on the stock and install the gun action.

REPAIRING STOCKS

In some cases you may wish to repair an old stock rather than replace or refinish it. If it merely has scratches or dents you can often conceal these quite easily. If the scratches are fairly shallow, use a colored wax stick such as found at building-supply places for patching furniture or paneling. This works best if you hold it in your hand for a bit to warm it. Then rub it over the scratch and buff with a soft cloth. These sticks are available in many colors; you match the color to the stock.

A larger hole or gouge can be repaired using shellac sticks. These are also available in all wood tones. To use, heat a small spatula, table knife, etc., over a smokeless flame such as a small alcohol burner. Then touch the heated blade to the shellac stick and quickly smear it in the gouge and smooth it down. Use extremely fine sandpaper or steel wool to buff down the area. Try to keep from cutting the finish around the area; however, if you do it can be touched up a bit with a good oil finish dabbed over the area with your finger, allowed to dry a bit, then buffed into the surrounding finish using fine steel wool.

A broken stock is another matter. You must be sure the stock will be safe for shooting after it has been repaired. A cracked or broken stock on a shotgun or rifle could be dangerous. On the other hand a small piece or sliver that has broken loose can often be glued back in place without any evidence of damage. If you wish to make the joint even more secure, you can also pin it with a wooden dowel or a screw covered with a dowel. Then fill and sand the dowel end down to fit the shape of the stock and spot-refinish to suit.

RESTOCKING

A more ambitious task is restocking a gun. This requires a fair amount of woodworking skills and tools in addition to some specialized tools. However, it is not a mysterious, hard-learned craft. Anyone with a bit of patience and the proper tools can learn to do this job. It is also one of the easiest, most satisfying ways of upgrading or customizing a gun. A fine old gun that you cherish but that has been beat against the sides of a duck blind or carries the scars of many a barbed-wire fence can be restored with a new stock. There are naturally other reasons for restocking a gun, such as a broken stock that can't be repaired, or one that doesn't fit properly. In some cases a stock can be altered to fit, but in many cases you'll do better with a new stock blank, shaped to fit the individual.

There are many stock blanks on the market. I recommend that you purchase a semi-inletted stock for your particular gun. Although you can purchase a blank and shape the stock to suit, this is quite a chore, and you can purchase almost any style and shape stock which has been rough-shaped on a duplicating lathe. The rough shaping

You can also purchase a semi-inletted replacement stock to replace a broken stock or customize your gun with a fancier stock. The factory inletting will be about 90 percent finished—usually more finished on shotgun stocks than on rifle blanks.

is about 90% of the chore of building a stock. Of course, if you want you can also purchase the blank and carve the stock yourself, but you'd better have a bit if experience in inletting factory stocks before you tackle this chore. Most factory stocks are about 90% inletted. This means you'll have to do a bit of work in fitting the action in place, but most of the work will be on the outside of the stock, rather than on the inside where the action fits in place. This isn't the case, however, with some sporterized rifle stocks.

Your first stock-replacement job would ideally be for a pump shotgun. These are the simplest to replace in terms of inletting work. In addition to the inletting, most factory stocks are about 5% large overall, so you can do any shaping, checkering, carving, etc. that needs to be done.

Selecting the Wood
Replacement stocks can be an economical piece of walnut, or they can be quite fancy, using exotic

woods such as crotch walnut. Often a fancy stock can upgrade a fine old gun with a worn factory stock, but don't make the mistake of putting a $100 stock on a $15 gun. No amount of "window dressing" will make the gun more valuable. Guns that have some antique value should also not be restocked unless absolutely necessary. You're better off dollar-wise if you repair and refinish the original, old stock.

Remarkably, two of the better stock manufacturers in the world are located in the same small town about 15 miles from my home. I have had the privilege of visiting their factories and looking at the curing kilns, and most of all drooling over a choice walnut stock. The hardest part of restocking a gun is in choosing the stock. There are so many different stock designs, woods, choices of wood grades, etc. that it becomes quite baffling at first. However, the best choice of walnut is French. It is harder and tighter and provides a more stable stock, which is extremely important in a fine sporter rifle. On the other hand, American walnut, which is a bit darker and redder, is the choice on almost all factory-sold rifles because it is a bit more economical. It will still hold true, and if the blank is chosen correctly can be as beautiful as French walnut. Other woods include maple, cherry, myrtlewood, and the laminated stock. I must be old-fashioned, but a laminated stock to me is like a neon sign. It just isn't natural.

The final sanding and finishing is the same for all gunstocks. However, the actual fitting can vary considerably depending on the type of gun and on its make.

Fitting the New Stock

Most of the modern pump and automatic guns, as well as some of the later-model doubles, have a

Note that although the action fits inside stock properly here, there is space between the action and stock. All wood and metal must fit properly for stock to withstand the abuse of recoil and to provide a safe-shooting gun.

Fit action to stock and mark areas that must be shaped to suit.

draw bolt through the butt. This is the easiest type of gun to fit a new stock to. The main thing is that the flat front portion of the stock must be inletted and shaped to fit perfectly to the flat rear area of the action. Then when the draw bolt is pulled up tight it will hold the two securely. This draw bolt should be checked before each season to make sure it hasn't become loose, or it can crack or damage the stock.

Most over-unders and some of the older doubles have the same basic joining requirements, al-

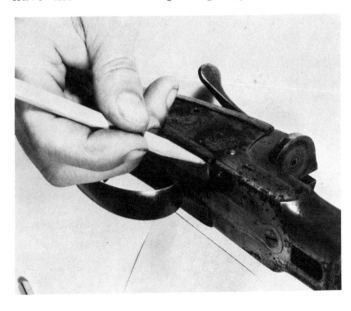

When stock will fit action, fit in place and fasten together. Then mark exterior portions of stock that must be removed. There should be a smooth blend of metal to wood.

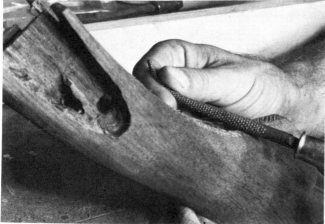

When stock and action fit properly, remove and shape rest of stock to suit, using appropriate rasps.

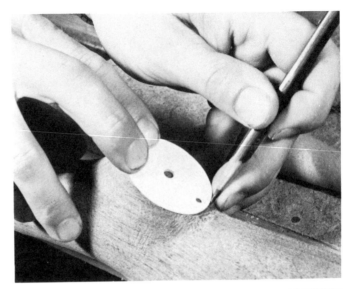

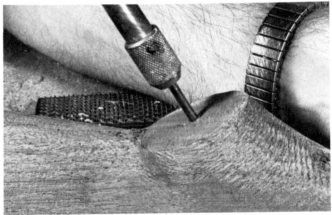

Installing the grip cap. First put the spacer in position and mark for removal of excess material. Mark and bore screw hole. Then fasten grip cap and spacer in place. Use small rasps to shape wood and grip cap to suit.

though they may vary a bit. It is extremely important with these guns to make sure the front of the stock fits properly to the rear of the action. There is normally less wood on these types of stocks, and unless this fit is perfect and done carefully, the small amount of contacting area will eventually cause stock problems from recoil. The fore-end on these guns should also be tightly fitted to prevent it from moving forward away from the action from the recoil. This is strictly a trial-and-error job. Rasp or chisel a little off the stock, then try the metal and wood together, again and again and again until you have a perfect fit. Painting the metal pieces with inletting paint will help by giving an indication of points of metal that are rubbing against the wood on the inside of the stock, or are keeping the metal portions from seating properly.

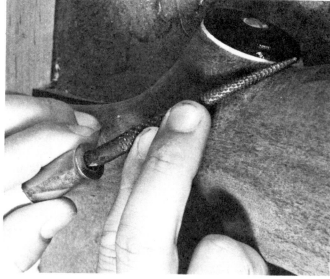

Because rifle stocks such as for bolt-action rifles present an entirely different set of problems, the complete carving, inletting, and bedding of a sporter stock are covered in Chapter 10 on customizing and sporterizing.

After you're satisfied with the inside fit of the stock to the metal, reassemble the gun entirely, and using a very fine pencil, mark the wooden portions that are protruding above the metal surfaces—for instance, at the action tang and around trigger guard. This is cut down in the same manner, a little at a time, fitting and cutting until you're satisfied. Although a chisel can be used to cut away portions that need a lot of wood removed, a couple of wood rasps—a cabinetmaker's rasp and a small round curved rasp—will suffice in most instances. Don't cut below the metal surface, but down almost flush; then the final sanding should bring the two flush.

Shape the rest of the stock to suit. For instance, you may wish to make a pistol grip smaller, or lower the comb.

For the final check, reassemble the gun and stock and make sure all metal blends in evenly with the wood and the stock is proportioned well and fits.

Sanding

Initial sanding should be done using 80-grit garnet paper. The best method of sanding is to fold the paper over a wood block which has been covered with a piece of old innertube. This can be used to smooth down the surface without causing uneven dips, or sanding spots. Make sure you sand with the grain; sanding across it will leave scratches in the stock that can be the devil to remove. After you have removed all file and machine marks, switch to 120-grit sandpaper and sand out the sanding marks left by the coarse sandpaper. Use sandpaper wrapped around your finger, a dowel, or even better yet a small section of air hose to sand areas around the cheekpiece, flutes of the point of the comb, etc.

It will take a bit of elbow grease, but eventually you'll have all the scratches out and a perfectly smooth stock. Don't skimp on this portion of the job. After you've spent this much time working on the stock, a sloppy job of sanding can mean wasted time and effort. Any areas that you don't get sanded completely will show up dark as the finish is absorbed by the scratches.

Finishing

There are many different gunstock finishes on the market, some good, some bad. Here are some suggestions on finishes from the Reinhart Fajen Gunstock Company, one of the leading gunstock manufacturers in the country.

There are several good finishes for gunstocks, and each has its points. Perhaps an oil finish is the most practical for the home workshop. Oil finish for most French walnut and plain American walnut works out very well. It seals the wood and if done well, gives the wood a beautiful warm glow. An oil finish is not completely waterproof, and if applied too hurriedly, may not dry hard. It does have a tendency to become tacky in warm humid weather, because of prolonged contact of moist cheek to finish.

An oil finish, if not completely dry, has a tendency to become dull with time, but it can be brightened up by rubbing in or polishing with another very light coat of oil.

There are several good gunstock finishing oils on the market. We have had good results with Tru-Oil and Linspeed. These will lessen some of the problems of an oil finish. Directions for using come with container. Be sure to let each *thin* application dry before applying the next coat.

If an oil finish is to be applied, the stock should be whiskered. This is a sanding process to remove grain ends that would eventually rise up and create a rough surface on the stock. If a lacquer, varnish, or plastic-type finish is to be used, this whiskering is not really necessary. To whisker, wet the surface of the stock with water, then dry quickly near heat of some kind. Ordinary room temperature will do, but may require thirty minutes or more depending on humidity and temperature. When the wood is dry, you will notice a roughness on the previously smooth surface. This is caused by the grain ends curling up. When thoroughly dry, these should be sanded off with 220-grit or finer sandpaper. Be sure to sand off only the grain ends; do not sand off the surface of the wood or you will uncover additional grain ends that should be whiskered.

One alternate method of developing a good oil finish is to use sanding sealer as the filler for *pores only*. Sanding sealer is sold as a sealer and filler under lacquer. It fills up the pores reasonably fast and is easily sanded off the surface of wood. Williams Gun Sight Company offers this sanding sealer in an aerosol spray can.

When the stock has been sanded to a fine finish, apply several coats of sealer and sand the sealer off the surface of the stock. When all pores have been built up level with the surface of the stock, carefully sand off any sealer remaining on the surface, being careful to not sand into the wood. This must be done so the oil can penetrate wood uniformly all over the stock.

For the first application, apply a generous amount of oil to the stock and allow it to penetrate the wood. Before it becomes too tacky or hard, wipe off all surplus oil. Allow this to dry. Then rub in a very small amount of oil every day or so until the desired luster develops. Do not build up a noticeable oil film on the surface. If this film builds up very much, the oil won't harden and will remain tacky.

Lecquer, varnish, vinyl, polyurethane, and epoxy spray-type finishes are clear, tough, and almost waterproof. The surface does not get tacky from perspiration when shooting in hot humid weather. Any of the above are harder than an oil finish and offer more protection to the wood. However, if the wood is scratched or dented, it can be more easily touched up in the average workshop when the original finish is oil.

A lacquer finish can be repaired by simply using the original method of finish application on the damaged area.

Some form of linseed-oil-base filler or plain linseed oil applied to walnut before applying the sealer or lacquer will give walnut that warm rich blend of color tones it is famous for. Be sure the filler or oil is dry and sanded off the surface of the wood and present only in the pores before applying the sealer or lacquer.

Surplus filler or oil should be wiped off before it dries; none should be left on the surface of the wood. The remaining film of filler or linseed oil can be sanded off the stock with fine sandpaper. Do not sand off any wood at this stage. Since the filler will clog sandpaper quickly, move to unclogged areas of sandpaper as it fills or use an open-coat paper.

When the pores of wood have been filled and sanded flush with wood, and given time to dry, the surface is ready for lacquer.

Epoxy or polyurethane finishes do not adhere well to filler- or oil-treated wood, so the finish itself is best used as the filler. On these materials, use instructions on container.

Lacquer and usually the synthetic finishes need to be sanded smooth to eliminate the "orange peel" or runs. The surface can then be polished to a high luster with Du Pont #7 Rubbing Compound.

Care must be exercised when sanding and polishing the finish that one does not cut through to the wood. These rubbed-through spots are sometimes hard to patch and blend in.

CHECKERING

One of the most challenging, exciting, satisfying, and often frustrating aspects of gun work is gun-

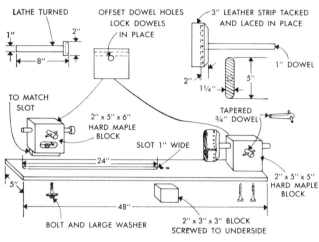

LATHE TURNED

OFFSET DOWEL HOLES
LOCK DOWELS
IN PLACE

3" LEATHER STRIP TACKED
AND LACED IN PLACE

1"   2"

8"

1" DOWEL

2"   1¼"   5"

TO MATCH
SLOT

2" x 5" x 6"
HARD MAPLE
BLOCK

SLOT 1" WIDE

TAPERED
¾" DOWEL

24"

2" x 5" x 5"
HARD MAPLE
BLOCK

5"

48"

BOLT AND LARGE WASHER

2" x 3" x 3" BLOCK
SCREWED TO UNDERSIDE

CHECKERING CRADLE

Use a checkering cradle to hold
the stock properly. You can make
your own.

stock checkering. Checkering is basically quite
simple. Although it takes a bit of practice to become adept at it, the techniques are actually easy
to learn.

Today's checkering is for pure decoration, but in
the early days it was used on swords and daggers
to provide a sure grip during battle. Today's modern stamped designs have nothing to do with pure
checkering. Although many of the fine guns of old
have extremely fine checkering, the most practical
checkering pattern for the home gun worker is 18
lines to the inch.

The only thing checkering really requires is a lot
of patience. It's a good idea to have the checkering
set up so it can be left, and you can work on it for
a half an hour or so then leave it when you become
tired. If you take your time and carefully follow the
correct steps, you can get a pretty fair checkering
job the first time. Then it becomes sort of addic-
tive. A friend of mine borrowed my tools to learn

how and I gave him an old stock for practice at the same time. He spent the entire week checkering, and he checkered the wooden knobs on the kitchen cabinet, the broom handle, and I think even a corner of the dining-room table before he was asked to leave the house.

For a good checkering job the work must be held securely. Although a vise will do, a homemade checkering cradle is much more convenient. By adjusting the movable clamping block you can fit the cradle to a rifle stock or shotgun stock of almost any size and shape.

You can practice checkering on almost any piece of wood, but it's best to practice on an old stock so you get the idea of working in the round rather than on a flat piece of wood.

The first step in checkering is to finish the stock, using a quality stock finish. However, don't apply the rubbing compound or wax yet, because you

If you wish to copy a checkering design, place a piece of thin paper over design and rub with soft pencil to make a "rubbing." Then transfer the outline to a piece of flexible cardboard and use it as a pattern. If pencil won't show on the finish, use a metal scribe.

will be applying a couple more coats of finish after the checkering is completed.

When the stock finish is completely dry, place the stock in the checkering cradle and position it securely. Select the pattern you feel is appropriate for your particular stock.

There are several patterns on the market for specific guns, or you can use one of the basic patterns, modifying it to fit your particular gun. You can also design your own pattern. Let's start with a fore-end pattern for your first checkering. Measure the points A, B, C, D on the stock and transfer this to a piece of tracing paper. Then draw lines connecting these points as shown. Now draw the center lines. Make a diamond template of a flexible piece of cardboard such as a file card. Sketch in the pattern you wish, using the diamond template for the ends, etc. This is called an angular pattern. Regardless of how you design the pattern, make sure the diamond pattern is used to establish the master lines of the pattern.

Another type of pattern is called a fill-in pattern, and this can have curved lines and shapes to fit the stock rather than the straight diamond angular lines. When the pattern suits, you're ready to make a template and transfer this to the stock. Use a sharp scriber to mark the master lines, and then lightly mark the border lines with dotted lines as shown. You will probably not come out perfectly on the dotted border lines using this type of pattern. If using a fill-in pattern, scribe the outline and master lines equally.

Making a pattern for a pistol grip is a bit harder because the curved portion of the stock won't allow the paper to fit it properly. One of the easiest methods of applying a pattern to a stock is to use one of the decal patterns on the market. These are designed by master gunsmiths and are available in patterns to fit almost any gun. In use they're simply placed on the stock and the checkering done right over the decal. Then when the checkering is finished, what is left of the decal can readily be washed off with soap and warm water.

Although you can purchase individual checkering tools, the best bet is to secure a good checkering set. It should have a V-cutter, a single-line cutter, a spacing cutter, a "router," and a flexible rule. In addition there are right-angle cutters, left-angled cutters, etc., but you'll seldom use these.

After the pattern has been established, use the

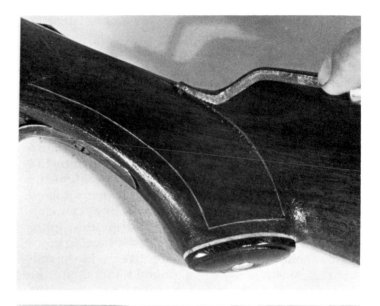

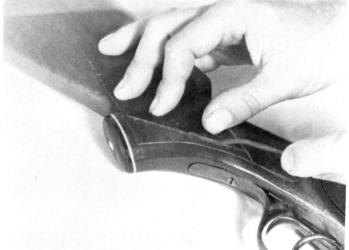

First step in checkering is to
deepen outlines using a single-
line tool or, better yet, a long
jointer. Then mark the main
lines, using a straightedge.

A marked pattern with main
lines.

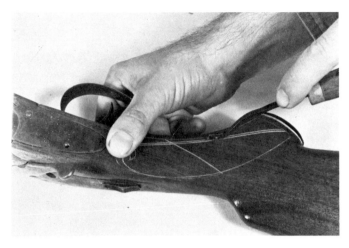

Deepen one of the main lines, then use a double-line spacer to start cutting the checkering. Allow the left hand side of the tool to fit down in groove already cut to mark and cut the groove on right side of line. Cut only about ¾ full depth at this time, continuing to cut all lines in one direction.

V-cutter to cut the master lines and the border lines to about ¹⁄₃₂ inch deep. Use extreme care in cutting these lines. For straight edges, I like to first score the line using a flexible straightedge and a single-line cutter or router, then follow with the V-cutter. This especially goes for the master lines. Again, don't cut the temporary border lines at this time. With master lines thoroughly marked and cut, place the spacer cutter with the left edge of the tool in the master line and cut a new line with the right edge of the cutter. Use short push-pull motions with the tool, keeping your arm in tight to your body. Don't hurry, and keep the lines straight. This is the hardest portion to learn, but like riding a bicycle, once you get the feel, you've got it. Keep the dust brushed out of the lines as you proceed. Don't worry about making lines full depth at this time—merely mark them good. Also, don't worry about going fully up to the border. This will be done later. The main thing is to be very careful when approaching the border. After a couple hours' work, one bad slip as you approach the border and you'll be a mighty sick craftsman.

Cut all the parallel grooves in one direction to about ¾ their full depth; this leaves a bit of flat top between each groove. Now turn the stock and use the same procedure on the second master line. As you cut you'll see the flat diamond appear. Continue cutting these grooves until you complete the pattern. Be careful not to cut so deeply into the wood that you break the diamonds or make the checkering appear uneven.

If you wish to add a bit more design to the checkering, use a skip-line spacer ,which produces the

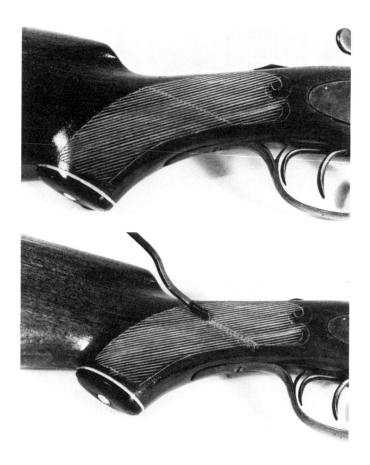

Once all lines in one direction have been cut, use spacer to cut all lines in opposite direction.

French checkering or skipped lines every so often in the pattern so the tops of the diamond disappear (except for the French checkering cuts) and the entire checkering is evenly cut.

Use a jointer tool to finish the lines at the border. The type of wood will determine how fast this step can be done. Naturally on hard, tight-grained woods the diamonds will hold their shape better; on soft woods you will have to proceed more slowly to maintain the proper diamond shape. Some gunsmiths like to use the V-tool to sort of "polish the cuts." Then last, deepen the border lines with the border tools. If you do happen to go over the border with a small slip, it can often be sanded and filed down a bit. Apply a coat of stock finish, rub the stock down, and polish thoroughly.

WOOD INLAYING

Wood inlaying used to be a tedious, arduous task that required very special tools and years of prac-

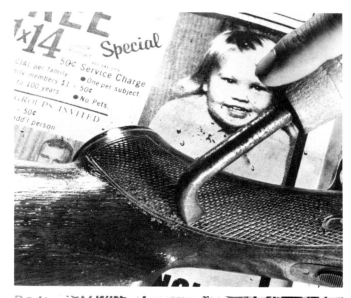

When all lines have been cut, deepen them to proper depth using a jointer or single-line spacer. This homemade checkering tool just can't be beat for finishing up the outside edges of checkering or working in small tight places.

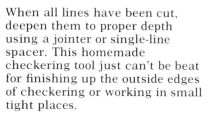

A border tool can be used to cut a border around the carving, eliminating many of the overruns you might have created.

tice to achieve. The old-time inlaying was done by cutting a design in the wood, then undercutting it slightly with tiny chisels. Then thin strands of silver or gold were driven into the undercuts and tamped down securely.

You can do your own silver or gold inlaying today with about a tenth the cost in money and time. The secret is in using a paste made up of silver or gold powder. Bob Brownell sells an excellent kit called a Bonanza Silver or Gold Kit. You still have to carve the channels using a tiny chisel. The V-chisel with your checkering set will do fine for the initial cuts, then you'll need to use a very sharp chip-carving knife to undercut the channels just a

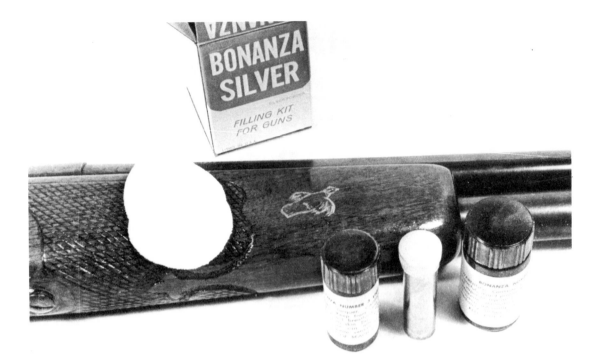

The materials required for silver inlaying are available in kit form from Brownell's, Inc.

First step is to transfer design to stock. Chalk on back of tracing paper is used.

bit. They don't have to be cut as much as in the old days because the silver paste will stay in place better than the solid silver. It's a good idea to also bore tiny holes along the channels to provide a "key." The liquid will flow into these holes and help hold the silver in place. If you're going to cover a fairly large area such as a small shield, etc., drive small brads down below the surface of the top of the shield. This will also help lock that

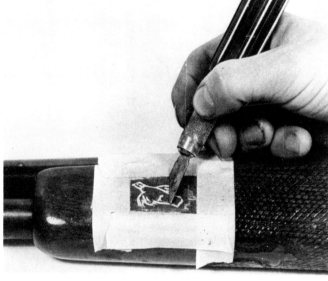

Once carving is completed and the area wiped with special cleaner, mix silver or gold paste according to instructions and apply it with a paper match. Clean away excess silver with a sharp knife.

area in place. The carving is strictly a woodworking job, but it looks a lot better if it is kept to simple delicate lines.

One of the main things is to make sure there are no open pores in the wood surrounding the inlay. The fine powder will fill any pores around the area as well as it will the carved design, and it's extremely hard to remove with steel wool. Once the carving is completed, use fine sandpaper or steel wool to knock down the rough edges left from the carving.

Then mix the powder and chemical bonding agent together according to the directions packaged with it. It should be about the consistency of

You can also make your own handgun stocks. Remove old stock and use as a pattern, or customize to suit. Cut out on bandsaw and shape with rasps and checker. Then cut stock apart to create right and left sides.

heavy cream. You want it to flow a bit, but not be runny. Using the cleaner furnished with the kit, wipe off the carving area. Using a toothpick, work the paste down in the inlay, making sure there are no bubbles, high spots, etc. Once you have the carved grooves filled with the paste, smooth them down with a tiny sliver of wood flattened on one end. Leave the paste a bit high, because it has a tendency to shrink somewhat. Let set overnight, then, using a very sharp knife, cut any ridges or high spots down flush with the wood surface. Small bits of excess silver around the area can be scraped away with a sharp razor. Then burnish the entire area with 4/0 steel wool and use a touch-up gunstock finish to blend the finish in with the surrounding finish. After the finish has been applied and dried, buff down with 4/0 steel wool and paste wax, then apply a good gunstock polish to the area.

If you're doing a large area such as a monogram, apply the silver in thin layers, allowing each to dry before applying the next.

MAKING HANDGUN GRIPS

Compared to other restocking problems making a new pair of grips for a handgun is a snap. You can purchase replacement stock grips of many different kinds of material, or make up your own from fancy woods. The methods are the same except for the techniques involved in sawing and shaping the different materials. The main thing in getting a good pair of grips is to choose a good hard tight-grained wood that will show checkering or carving well. Choose a blank thick enough so you can make both grips from it. You can make a duplicate pair of grips or make up a pair to suit your hand better, depending on your choice.

If you're making a pair of duplicate grips, remove the old grips, place them on the grip blank, clamp, and drill for the holding screws and escutcheon plate. Fasten the old grips to the grip blank with a screw or pin through the screw holes, then mark around the old grip. This way you'll have a grip that will fit perfectly. Cut around the grips with a coping saw or bandsaw, then place the grip blank in a vise and cut down the middle to saw apart the two different grips.

Shape, checker, and finish in the same manner as a stock. If you wish to customize the grip to suit, you can drop melted wax onto your old grips, then use a sharp knife to cut away the material to suit. Use this as a pattern to custom-design your own handgun grips.

CHAPTER FIVE

REBLUING AND METALWORK

Gun metalwork, as the old saying goes, separates the men from the boys. Much of it requires specialized tools and techniques. There are many jobs that shouldn't be tackled by the inexperienced home gun worker, such as rechambering and headspacing. Such jobs should be left to the boys with the big shops and years of experience. On the other hand, there is a great deal of metalwork that can be done safely, starting with the simplest chores such as rust removal, touch-up bluing, and making small parts. It's a good idea to practice on old guns or gun parts first to learn the techniques. In fact, some slight metalwork on old guns can often make them much more attractive as well as provide a good learning experience. Even if they're not safe to fire, the results can make a fine mantelpiece or office decoration—but remove firing pins before displaying these guns.

REMOVING STUBBORN OR RUSTY SCREWS

One of the hardest chores a gun worker can have is removing a stubborn or rusty screw. The first step in dealing with any screw, stuck or not, is to choose the correct screwdriver. The screwdriver should fit the screw-head slot perfectly, even if the screwdriver has to be ground to fit. A screwdriver with a parallel-side blade works best for this type of work. Not only will the blade "bottom" perfectly

A ratchet-handle screwdriver can be used sometimes, but be careful not to twist the screw head off.

in the slot, but more of the screwdriver blade contacts the screw-head slot to distribute the pressure. A screwdriver with a ratchet attachment can be used to provide more torque to the screwdriver. However, on smaller-size screws you'll probably bend or break the screwdriver blade before you turn the screws.

There are a couple of things you can do to help loosen stuck screws. The first is to use Liquid Wrench to help cut away rust and loosen materials such as varnish or Loctite which are used in scope-mounting screw holes to help prevent the screws from working loose.

You can also help loosen some screws by tapping the screwdriver in the screw slot. This sometimes drives the screw forward, providing enough movement to allow the screw to become loosened. After these methods have been applied, then use the screwdriver with a ratchet attachment. First make sure the gun or part is locked securely in a vise so you have both hands free to hold the screwdriver properly in position. It should be held tightly down in the slot with one hand, and straight up and down, not tipped to one side or the other. Then use the other hand on the ratchet to slowly try to remove the stubborn screw.

Although experts often loosen a screw by heating the surrounding metal, it's not a job for the average gun worker. For instance, it takes a temperature of about 400° to affect substances such as Loctite. By the time you reach that temperature the hardness will have been drawn from virtually all metals.

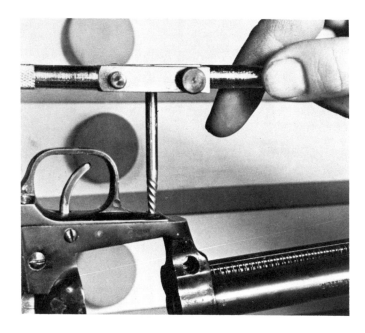

A screw that is broken can sometimes be taken out by using a screw extractor.

REMOVING A BROKEN SCREW

Use all caution to prevent breaking off a screw head or screw, because once you do, it may be almost impossible to remove, and may have to be done by a professional. Broken screw heads or screw bodies in larger open pieces can sometimes be removed with a screw extractor. If not, they will have to be drilled out (making sure both pieces are properly drilled), then the holes retapped for a new and larger screw.

Drilling and tapping are discussed in detail in Chapter 6.

RUST REMOVAL

One of the worst problems that plague guns is rust. Interior portions of guns can often be derusted with one of the rust-removing formulas on the market, merely soaking the parts in the remover, then steel-wire-brushing off the rust and reoiling. Or as mentioned in the chapter on cleaning, the parts can often be boiled clean, then reoiled. Rust removal on exteriors, however, particularly on blued surfaces, presents an entirely different problem. If the gun has a good heavy coating of bluing one of the best methods of rust removal is merely lots of elbow grease with 4/0 steel wool. Surprisingly, you won't cut the bluing on a good blue job, but will remove tiny rust spots if they're not already too deeply pitted into the metal. In that case you may have to completely tear down the gun, strip off the rust and blue, then polish and reblue the gun.

REBLUING

For years gun writers and gunsmiths have been saying the only way to get a good blue job is with the hot-bluing method, utilizing lots of equipment such as tanks and heaters, and that this should be done only by an experienced gunsmith. True, many a fine gun has had a streaked unsightly finish applied by a novice, but often the reason for the bad blue job was poor preparation of the metal before the bluing was applied and not the blue coating itself. You can do a good job of bluing in a home gun shop without a lot of expensive equipment using either a cold- or a hot-bluing method, but it takes a lot of work and not a little patience to get that professional-looking finish. There are probably more formulas for bluing guns than there are fleas on a stray pup, many of them dreamed up by a gun tinkerer. Some work, and others are about as good as stove polish.

Careful preparation is the key to the velvet-smooth blue job. Even if you don't wish to tackle a full bluing job, you can strip the metal clean, polish it, reoil it, and take it to a gunsmith for the actual bluing. All he has to do then is degrease and blue the gun. You can spend more time than he can on the preparation, and normally you'll end up with a better blue job. Make sure you wire all parts

Although cold bluing has been condemned by many gun writers for years, the bluing materials offered today can provide a fine blue job.

The main thing regardless of the method of bluing is proper preparation of the surface. First step is to apply a cleaner-degreaser. Then strip off old blue, using a blue remover.

together that will be blued so none will become lost during transit.

Preparation for Bluing

Regardless of what method of bluing is to be used, the first step is to disassemble the gun and apply a cleaner-degreaser, using a soft cloth. Have plenty of rags on hand for the job. Then strip off the old blue, using a good blue and rust remover. This will strip the surface down to the bare gray metal. Make sure you get the stripper down in all crevices. The gun should be completely torn down for a good job and the stock removed. Use cotton swabs for the tight spots. Then use a fine-grit abrasive cloth to work out the rust and pits. If the rust spots are deeply pitted, use 400-grit wet or dry paper to polish them out. The novice may polish or "sand" off the sharp edges of the metal, leaving

The metal surface must be cleaned and polished. This can be done with abrasive papers, or you can use a steel wire wheel if you're careful not to cut down corners or edges.

Once the part is cleaned and degreased, it must not be touched by your hands or you will leave oily fingerprints that can ruin the blue job. Use wooden plugs or your fingers placed in barrel.

an unsightly appearance. Use wood blocks, metal files, or anything you can find to wrap the paper around to maintain the correct metal surface. If you have a wire wheel on a bench grinder, it can be used to cut down the rust pits a lot faster than hand sanding, but you've got to be mighty careful not to cut into the metal too much in one area or round off edges or corners. This is one chore that should definitely be practiced on an old gun before you attempt it on one of your good guns. Keep the wheel running lengthwise with the metal. Don't make cross strokes on the receiver or barrel. Take your time and examine often to make sure you're getting the pits out, but are not cutting off too much metal. One of the most important parts of metal preparation for bluing is to have the tiny cuts made by the abrasive cloth or wire wheel running lengthwise with the metal.

Once all pits have been removed, polish the metal thoroughly, using 400-grit steel wool. Once the metal is polished you're ready for the bluing. The metal is completely unprotected at this point, so if you need to stop for a bit, or plan to take the gun to a gunsmith for the bluing, apply a light coat of oil to all metal surfaces. If you plan on doing the bluing yourself, from now on the metal surface mustn't be touched by your fingers or you'll leave oily fingerprints that can ruin a blue job. Insert a wooden plug in the barrel so it can be handled, wire small parts together, and handle receivers by their bolts or tang. Clean and degrease all parts thoroughly, using a good cleaner-degreaser applied with a clean cloth. Then wipe off with a clean dry soft cloth or rinse under water, being careful not to touch the metal with your hands.

Cold Bluing
The biggest problem in applying cold bluing is to get it on quickly, yet evenly. It starts forming the coloring almost the instant it hits the metal. The

streaks and smears sometimes seen on cold-bluing jobs are the result of not applying the bluing fast enough, or leaving some areas uncovered while others are flooded. Apply the liquid or paste bluing, using a soft cotton swab or cloth, and apply it confidently, smearing it down as evenly as possible and as quickly as possible. Use long smooth strokes with the bluing. On a gun barrel move from one end to the other without stopping. Allow the solution to stay on the metal for no more than 30 to 60 seconds, or following the manufacturer's instructions, then wipe it off with a dry cloth if using paste blue. If the bluing is liquid, rinse it away with cold water. Then polish with 4/0 steel wool.

If the coating appears uneven in some areas, merely recoat with a second, third, or even fourth coat of bluing until the metal takes on a deep even color. Then polish well with steel wool and finally give all metal surfaces a coating of protective oil.

Hot Bluing

Regardless of whether you're doing a hot-bluing or cold-bluing job, the metal preparation is the same. Although it's not feasible for the average gun owner to have all the equipment of a large shop for hot-bluing guns, he can do a bit of "kitchen stove" bluing that will give a surprisingly good result. The coloring is much more evenly applied than with the cold bluing and in my opinion is one of the best "home-applied" blues.

The bluing material comes in a kit from Herter's and is called Belgian Blue. It comes complete with bluing, cleaner, a small boiling tank, and abrasive cloth for around $6. It will do one or two rifles or shotguns. However, to be on the safe side, order an extra bottle of bluing.

This type of hot bluing won't effect the solder on double-barrel shotguns or barrel ribs. The main difference between this type of bluing and gun-shop bluing is the time and effort required to do the job. However, with care and good preparation you can apply a deep black-blue that's comparable to the finest factory blue.

After preparing the metal as before, make a wooden barrel plug to fit the barrel, or two plugs for a double-barrel. Although the bluing solutions won't harm the barrel, they do have a tendency to blue it, and the plugs also make it easier to handle the gun during the procedure. You will also need

Using a special bluing kit from Herter's, you can also hot-blue guns.

In addition to the bluing kit, you will also need household lye, distilled water, and a pair of clean white cotton gloves.

some bent wire hooks and clean white cotton gloves for removing the metal pieces from the hot water and handling during the cleaning process. The cotton gloves help keep fingerprints off the metal after it has been cleaned. Any fingerprints at this time will show up in the bluing.

Add a tablespoonful of household lye to 2½ gallons of rainwater or distilled soft water and bring to a slow rolling boil. The water must be boiled in a container long enough to hold the gun barrel you will be bluing. These can be purchased from Herter's, or if you live in a rural area check at a local feed store for a chicken-feed or watering trough. Whatever the utensil, place it over two burners of your kitchen stove.

When the solution is slowly boiling, place the gun parts in it and allow to boil for about thirty minutes. Keep it boiling with a slow rolling boil so it doesn't boil wildly and boil over. The solution is caustic, so wear old clothes, goggles, and heavy cotton gloves during the procedure.

The gun has now been degreased and it's advisable to have all other materials on hand to finish the job, as the gun is extremely susceptible to rusting at this time.

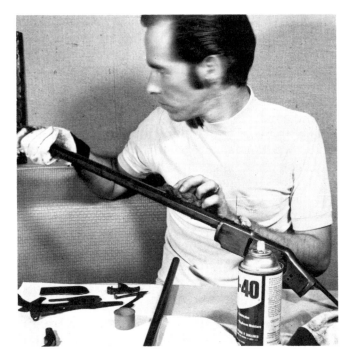

Remove gun parts and wipe with bluing solution using a cotton swab. It may take as many as fifteen or twenty coats for a good coating. Allow to dry, then steel-wool between coats with 4/0 steel wool.

Place the gun parts on clean newspapers or hang them up, being careful not to touch them with your bare hands.

Empty out the lye water with all due caution and rinse out the tank. Then place it back on the stove and fill with clean rainwater or distilled water. Ordinary tap water won't work. Remove the cap from a bottle of Belgian blue and place it in one corner of the bluing tank. This will allow the bluing solution to heat at the same time as the water does. *Make sure that the water can't boil over into the bottle.* Use a larger bottle than the one it came in if necessary. Then place the cleaned gun parts in the tank and bring the water to a slow rolling boil and again boil for about thirty minutes.

Place a double layer of newspapers on the kitchen table or work area and remove one gun part at a time, using wire hooks. The metal will flash-dry the instant you remove it from the hot water. Holding the part with the wire or clean cotton gloves, coat it the instant it dries with the Belgian blue, using a clean cotton swab. Apply the bluing in long even strokes going the length of the metal pieces. Make sure the coating is evenly applied. Set aside or hang up to dry and remove another part. After all parts have been coated once, use 4/0 steel wool to remove the rust particles that have formed. Do not rub too vigorously at this time or you will remove the thin coating of blue. Then place the parts back in the hot water and boil them for another three to seven minutes and again remove one at a time and coat them the instant they dry. Rub with steel wool when all parts have been coated.

The first coats of bluing will appear a dull grayish brown, but as more coats are applied the bluing will take on a deep, dark, blue-black appearance. In some cases you may be able to get by with ten coats of bluing. However, depending on the steel used, you may also need to apply as many as twenty, heating, applying solution, rubbing down with steel wool, and then boiling again.

After the last coating of bluing, rub down with steel wool to remove excess rust, then place parts back in the boiling water and allow them to boil for ten minutes or more. Remove parts from the boiling water and allow them to set overnight. Then apply light oil and you're finished.

Some small parts won't blue quite as well as others using this method, because they cool down rapidly once removed from the heat. To prevent this, heat them a bit longer. Make sure you have a good light in the area you're doing the bluing, so you can examine each coat thoroughly as it is applied and rubbed down.

Heat Bluing
Small parts such as metal screws can be blued by the use of heat. In fact this is the method that Colt and Smith & Wesson have used to achieve such a deep-blue luster in the past. However, the heat bluing they did was done in a large oven. Heat bluing in the home shop is merely heating the gun part in open flame until it turns a deep blue. A second method is to heat the metal to about 700°

Small parts such as screws can often be blued by applying heat, then buffing with fine steel wool.

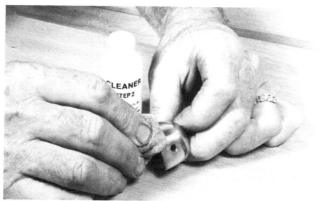

Pieces to be plated are steel-wooled or polished with wire wheel, and buffed to a satin shine with buffing compound. Then cleaner from kit is applied and the part is dipped in distilled water and allowed to dry.

to 1000°, then quench it in linseed oil mixed with Hoppe's No. 9 Solvent.

PLATING

Some small plating jobs such as a trigger and end cap can be handled using one of the smaller plating kits available from mail-order gunsmithing-supply houses. Larger jobs such as plating an entire revolver should be left to the professionals. You can, however, prepare the metal in the same manner as you would for bluing, then take the gun to the professional for plating.

If you wish to try your hand at electroplating on a small scale, you might wish to gold-plate a trigger. It's fun, there is not a heck of a lot of dough involved, and you can dress up your favorite gun quite easily in this manner. Although there are several different small plating kits on the market, they all work basically the same. The metal is first wire-brushed to remove all rust, pits, etc., then buffed and polished on a cloth wheel, using progressively finer grits of polishing compound until it is shiny and polished to mirror finish. The metal is then cleaned with cleaner supplied in the kit. From this point on the part must be handled with pliers or tweezers to prevent getting oily fingerprints on the cleaned metal surface. Then the item

Plating unit shown is hand-held, utilizes plating solution and pen batteries.

is plated by immersing in a solution which is supplied with low voltage electricity. There are different plating solutions for gold, silver, etc. (In most instances you will have to plate with copper first.) Some smaller units may utilize a "plating gun," which is filled with solution, utilizes a battery to keep the solution "working," and has a felt tip for applying the solution.

With the plating solution applied, the next step is to wash it off in distilled water and polish with a clean cloth wheel.

BLACKING

Although there are hot blacking formulas which were used on many different military guns in previous times, they have largely fallen out of favor. Today blacking is primarily used to repair a finish on brass, bronze, or copper (or aluminum such as scopes), to blacken swivels, etc., and on some shotgun receivers.

These are applied according to instructions on the label of the bottle. In most instances metal must be cleaned with cleaning solvent or cleaner degreaser much in same manner as for bluing.

BROWNING

Today a browned finish is associated mostly with muzzleloaders, but in days past it was used on many guns and was one of the first "gun finishes." It is nothing more than controlled rusting of the metal surface. There are several different browning formulas on the market. One of the best is marketed in kit form by Birchwood Casey for finishing muzzleloaders. Again the old finish is removed and the metal is polished and degreased. Then in the

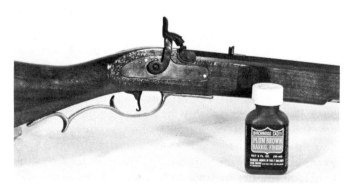

A brown finish, which is nothing more than controlled rusting such as used on muzzleloaders, can be applied as easily as the cold bluing. The same careful metal preparation is necessary.

case of the brown finish the gun barrel is suspended over a heat source and allowed to heat until the barrel is hot enough so that a drop of water sizzles on it. The browning solution is then applied quickly with a clean cotton swab and allowed to set for ten minutes or so. Then the barrel is rinsed in clean water, wiped dry with a steel cloth, and polished with steel wool. Darker coloring is achieved by applying more coats. Finally, polish with steel wool and apply oil to preserve the finish.

If you want to be stubborn, however, you can make up your own "old-time" browning solution, although the ease with which the kits work makes mixing your own a bit ridiculous. The solution can be made up of:

¾ oz. spirits of nitre
¾ oz. tincture of steel
¼ oz. crude sulfur
½ oz. blue vitriol
¼ oz. corrosive sublimate
1 drachm nitric acid
¼ oz. copperas

Mix in a pint of distilled water. Keep in a glass jar with a glass lid to keep the fumes from rusting surrounding metal. To use, merely wipe on the barrel and allow to set for about thirty minutes, then burnish with steel wool. Apply as many coats as needed.

Old-fashioned browned finishes were protected with a coat of either beeswax or linseed oil after the browning process was neutralized by boiling the part in water and then allowing it to flash-dry. You can also rust metal using a 10 percent solution of salt in water, but it takes quite a bit of time.

SOLDERING

Some soldering jobs should be left to the experts, for instance when an entire rib comes loose from a good double-barrel shotgun. On the other hand if only a small portion of one end of the rib is loosened you can often solder it back in place without a heck of a lot of trouble.

To many, soldering is one of those mysterious arts that seems more complicated than it's worth. And if you start to purchase soldering materials you'll literally be pulling your hair wondering what should be used for what. Like many things, however, it can be as simple or complicated as you want. Solder is basically an alloy of tin and lead, and it comes in many different "hardnesses"—or rather melting points—which are determined by the amount of tin or lead in the solder.

Soft Soldering

For most home gun work you can forget about the mathematics of figuring what solder should be used for what, although in a working shop different melting points are used for different jobs. For most work a 50-50 solder is fine. It contains 50% tin and 50% lead, and has a melting point of 401.0°. It should be purchased in solid wire or strips. Forget the hollow, flux-filled solder; it's more trouble than it's worth. In most cases the wire solder can be used quite effectively. However, sometimes you will need tiny thin strips of solder. In this case merely hammer the wire down flat, scrape away the dirty surface, and you're ready for action.

You will also need soldering flux. This is used to coat the metal surface to be soldered. It prevents premature oxidation, which happens when the metal surface is heated, and also helps flush impurities from the surface as it flows away. It can be purchased in either paste or liquid form. There are many different fluxes on the market, but the one that seems to work the best for me is Brownell's Tix solder and flux. It's a good idea to purchase the flux and solder together to make sure they're compatible.

An easier method of soldering utilizes a paste "Fusion Solder" which is solder ground up in its own flux. This is available in all different temperatures, including soft, hard, and silver-soldering materials. Brownell's carries a full line of soldering materials and their catalog describes quite simply what each should be used for.

Although many different heat sources can be utilized for soldering, my favorite is a hand-held propane torch. Purchase one of these with the two sizes of torch tip and you can have pretty fair control of the flame size, which is important in gun soldering.

Soldering takes a bit of practice and you'd better not try it for the first time on a fine gun. Use an old gun or a couple of pieces of scrap metal for practice first. The most important thing in soldering is cleanliness. If done properly, soldering can be so simple it is amazing. If done wrong, it can be more frustrating than a bird-dog pup with your Sunday newspaper. The first step is to clean the

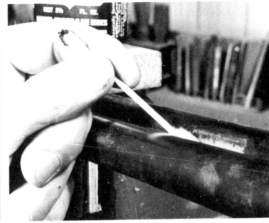
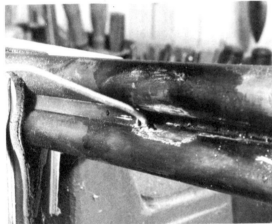

For soldering, metal must be cleaned thoroughly down to bare metal, using an abrasive cloth, a tiny file, or steel wool. Then degrease the metal thoroughly. A gun scrubber or degreaser can be used for this, or lacquer thinner (do this out in the open). Tin the metal surface by first coating with the proper flux, then heating the metal slowly until a bit of solder will flow in place to coat the metal surface. This must be done to both surfaces of metal that will be contacting. Then clamp the two pieces together and heat each equally so the solder will melt and flow between them.

metal thoroughly. All old solder, bluing, rust, etc. should be cut away, using about 140-grit, open-coat aluminum-oxide cloth. In some cases you may even have to file a bit of material away. Make sure the area is cleaned down to bare metal. If it's not, the solder absolutely won't stick. This is one of the most important steps in a good solder joint. Once you have the joint cleaned, don't touch it with your finger or use any solution on it or you may contaminate it. There are basically two methods of soldering: tinning and by capillary action. In the tinning method, the area, for instance the barrel of a gun for a ramp sight, is first marked with a lead pencil. Then, using a strip of sanding cloth, sand the metal down thoroughly, making sure you don't get out of the penciled outline of the ramp. Sometimes I find that a tiny flat file does a better job than the cloth strip because the cloth has a tendency to wrap around the barrel. But make sure you don't cut into the metal—merely clean the surface with the file. With the metal cleaned, tin the surface of the barrel. To do this, first coat the surface with flux, using a small flux brush. Then heat the metal slowly, not directly on the area to be soldered but entirely around it, until a bit of solder will flow onto the surface. The major trick in soldering is to heat the metal enough so it will melt the solder, instead of directly heating the solder, which results in a "cold solder joint" that holds about as well as chewing gum. When the solder melts and runs over the surface, use the flux brush to quickly brush it in place. Then use a soft clean cloth to wipe away excess solder before it melts. Now you have the barrel tinned. Repeat the same steps on the ramp. Allow each to cool thoroughly, then coat both surfaces with a bit of flux. Clamp the two pieces together solidly, making sure they're in proper position. Then heat the two pieces equally, playing the flame around the entire area, not holding it in one spot. When the heated metal heats the solder to the proper melting temperature, it will flow, bonding the two pieces together. And that's how simple it is.

Incidentally, a bit of soldering talc rubbed around the area will prevent solder from sticking to the areas you don't want it, or you can also use a soft pencil, as the graphite from the lead will do the same thing. Quickly wipe away any excess solder that has been squeezed out with a soft clean cloth. A touch-up with solder black can darken any fine line of solder that shows around the joint.

Capillary-action soldering is done a bit differently and requires a bit more experience. It is about the only method of soldering solid ribs to older shotguns. One of the paste-solder fluxes works pretty well for this job. The parts are cleaned and fluxed as before, then clamped securely. Soldering talc or graphite is used to cover surrounding metal to prevent solder from sticking where it isn't wanted. The barrel or barrels are heated slowly until they will melt the solder, then it is applied quickly to the one side of the rib, holding the flame tip on the opposite side. The heat draws the solder down into the joint. Quickly switch to the opposite side and solder it in the same manner.

Hard Soldering

Hard soldering is accomplished in much the same manner as soft soldering, although the melting temperature is higher and the resulting tensile strength is higher. One of the best hard solders on the market is Hi-Force 44. It comes with its own flux and is available from most gunsmithing supply houses.

Silver Soldering

Silver solder is probably used for more gun work than any other kind of solder. Many consider it a hard solder; however, it is actually a composition of silver, and other metals depending on the melting temperature needed. Although silver soldering can be done with a propane torch, it's best done with an oxyacetylene torch. One of the small units will handle most any gun work that you will need to do. Again, selection of the proper solder is most important. Silver solder used for jewelry work or even that used by plumbers for copper pipes won't do as well as that offered for gunsmithing work by the gunsmithing supply houses. Silvaloy along with its compatible flux is the best choice for gun work. It is available in flat strips, and two sizes of wire. I've found that flat strips work the best, because they can be cut and filed to any shape needed. In silver-soldering work the flux is also used as an indicator as to when to apply the solder. When it turns to a syrupy-brown consistency the solder can be applied.

Some silver solders can be dangerous because they give off fumes that can make you seriously ill or even kill you. In the quantities used in most gun work this wouldn't be a problem, but it's a good idea to have plenty of ventilation during the job.

Silver solder is used in both the tinning and the capillary-action methods. Silver solder should be used for soldering ramps on high-power rifles. (Soft solder is OK on .22s.) One of the tips to making good solder joints is to use as little solder as possible to do the job.

BRAZING AND WELDING

Although brazing can often be done on a gun, in most cases, particularly home gun work, silver solder will do as good a job without quite as much fuss. By the same token, welding is a job for the professionals unless you already have the equipment and knowledge. It takes a long time and plenty of dough to learn to weld properly, and so the occasional job you might do on your guns can be farmed out much more easily to a professional shop. Incidentally, you're much better off having a professional gunsmith shop do the welding than taking it down the road to a neighbor, because of the necessity of understanding the safety problems inherent in welded gun parts.

MAKING SMALL PARTS

Occasionally the gun worker will come up against the problem of replacing a part that isn't readily available. And that's where the fun comes in. With a little tinkering and patience many parts, such as springs and firing pins, can easily be made in your home shop. You can also make many of your own tools. Round parts can be made of steel drill rod and flat parts from flat stock of the right thickness. If you're looking for metal stock, go to a machine shop or welding shop and ask to look around in their scrap pile. You'll probably be welcome to clean it up for the asking, as the small pieces you require for making gun parts won't be missed by the machinist or welder.

First step in building a flat metal piece is to select the proper thickness metal, then coat it with layout paint. If the original part has a hole in it, bore a hole in the new stock to match and fasten the two pieces together, using pins. Then mark around the outside outline. Remove the original

First step in making a small part is to bore around the outline of the piece. Item can then be punched out of metal and shaped with a file.

part, centerpunch a series of holes around the outline, and using a drill press, drill small holes around the outline so they just touch each other. The part then can be broken out and filed or ground to shape.

Hardening

If the part must be heat-treated or hardened, heat it in a forge, in a heat-controlled furnace, or with a torch until it turns cherry red (the color between 1450° and 1650°). Then dip or roll in a hardening agent such as Kasenit or Hard-n-Tuff (both available from gunsmith supply houses), making sure the temperature is not allowed to drop between the heating and contact with the hardening compound. Make sure the area to be hardened is well covered. Allow the part to stay in the compound for about a minute so it will form a crust on the metal and fuse into it. Then return to the flame or furnace and heat until the compound fuses into the metal at a cherry-red heat. Watch carefully to make sure the metal is heated thoroughly and is ready to quench. If there is any doubt as to the result, repeat heating and dipping, then reheating until you're sure of the results. Then quench immediately in water or brine for low-carbon steels.

To case harden a part, heat it with a torch until it's cherry red, dip it in hardening agent, again heat it to a cherry red, and quench it immediately in water.

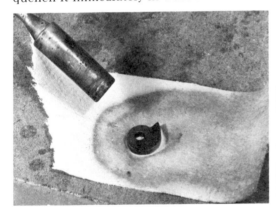

CHAPTER SIX

INSTALLING SIGHTS AND SIGHTING IN

How you install, maintain, and care for the sights on your gun can determine whether it will be a joy to shoot, or a frustration that sometimes gets thrown into the brush. Of course, it's often too easy to blame it on the gun—"Guess my sights must have been knocked off this morning." Many times that is indeed the case. However, you can't just get out your hammer and start adjusting sights without a little basic knowledge of exactly how they should work.

An incident on my neighbor's range last fall proved the point. A couple of friends were going to sight in their deer rifles. Both guns had just been taken down from the wall and hadn't been fired since the deer season before. The first shooter made a grouping shot, made a minute adjustment on the rear sight, and fired a quite satisfactory second group. His buddy shot three times and missed the backstop with two shots. He immediately went to his car and came back with a nail, a hammer, and an old screwdriver. He went to pounding his sights back and forth, shooting a single shot each time, only to end up an hour later a very frustrated shooter.

There were several things to learn from the incident. The first shooter had a good set of sights on his gun. Some guns come from the factory with satisfactory sights, others should have better sights installed. The first hunter also had sights that were

Most modern rifles are predrilled for scopes. The Williams Sight-Thru Mount gives the 742 Remington (shown above) both a scope for long-range shooting and an aperture for quick snap shooting at running game. Another type of scope mount by Williams fits the Model 94 Winchester (right), which is top-ejecting.

suited to him. Not everyone can use a peep sight, nor by the same token can some shooters tolerate a scope sight. Each sight must be suited to the gun, the shooter, and the situation. The third and most important factor is that the first shooter knew his sights and how to adjust them properly and how to properly sight in his gun.

Naturally, accuracy is largely dependent on the sights on a gun. The first step in improving accuracy is to replace cheap hard-to-adjust sights with good-quality, easily adjustable sights. These are available in a number of kinds and styles. Choose the type that suits you the best. It's a good idea to shoot a number of guns with different types of sights to determine the particular type of sight that suits you best.

Many sights can be installed or replaced with simple tools.

Almost all guns manufactured today, as well as some of the earlier ones, are drilled and tapped for standard telescope mounts or receiver sights. The only thing necessary to change to better sights is to remove the dummy screws plugging the holes and install the sight or sight mount with the screws furnished.

MOUNTING A SCOPE ON A GUN WITH SIGHT BASE OR MOUNT SCREW HOLES

The first step is to select the proper scope mount bases. There is a large variety of bases available, either one-piece or two-piece, depending on the gun, scope, etc. Most gun dealers will have charts that make selection of the proper mount bases easy. There are split-ring mounts, detachable top and side mounts, pivot mounts which allow you to quickly use either open or scope sights, etc.

Place the rifle in a good padded vise. Then level the rifle both ways. Using the proper-size screwdriver, remove the filler screws. Use cleaner-degreaser to remove all oil from the holes. Position the base or bases in place, and fasten with screws supplied. Put a bit of Loctite on the screw threads

Once dummy screws are removed from a predrilled rifle, place mounting blocks in position on barrel and dab a bit of Loctite on screws which come with mounting bases, then turn screws in place, using proper-size screwdriver. Lightly tapping on butt of screwdriver with your hand or a small hammer will get the screws tighter.

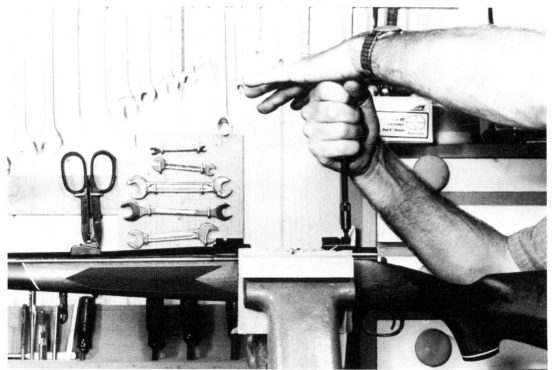

On a split-ring set, the bottom rings are first mounted on the bases and the scope is placed in position. Then the top rings are placed over the scope. Make sure scope fits in rings properly and is square with rifle horizontal and vertical so cross wires in scope line up with rifle bore, then screw rings down securely, tightening each screw a few turns at a time. Eye relief, or distance from end of scope to eyebrow or shooter's glasses, should be 3⅜ inches for high-powered rifles, about 2 inches for .22 rifles.

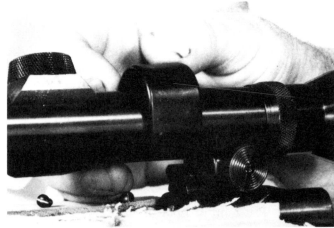

to help hold them in place. Use only the proper-size screwdriver. The screw handle should be fairly large, and the blades hardened. The importance of good, tight screws can't be stressed enough. A rifle scope takes a great amount of recoil and unless it is properly installed it will never stay accurate.

As you tighten the screw, tap on the end of the screwdriver with a plastic-faced hammer to help drive the screws tightly in place. Before final tightening of the scope-holding rings, position your face on the comb of the stock and sight through the scope. Slide the scope forward or backward to achieve the proper eye relief. You should be able to see the full field through the scope at the same time. There should be at least ⅛ inch between the ring and any projecting surface of the scope such as the objective bell or the power-selector ring. Also check to ensure that the reticle is level horizontally. Then tighten the ring screws. If it is a split ring, make sure both sides have the same amount of gap.

One of the main things in high-powered guns is to ensure that there is the proper amount of eye relief. It should be at least 3⅝ inches, preferably more, to prevent injury to the shooter from the recoil. This is especially important to shooters who wear glasses.

Normally .22 scopes will have a much shorter eye relief, about 2 inches.

MOUNTING SIGHTS OR BASES ON RIFLES WITHOUT FACTORY-BORED HOLES

Old military rifles such as the Springfield, Enfield, Mauser, and Remington M1903A3, which are often converted into sporter rifles, don't have prebored sight-base holes, so they must be drilled and tapped. Using a good set of taps and drills, a drill press, and the proper holding tools, plus jigs for drilling and tapping such as are made by the B-Square Company, the job can usually be done by even a first-timer without too much frustration. The problem comes in with the extremely hard receivers such as the old low-numbered Springfields, some of the Enfields, and the '03A3. Sometimes the case-hardened receivers of these guns can be real buggers. A good test of the hardness of the receiver is to run a sharp file across it. If the file won't cut the receiver, you're in for some

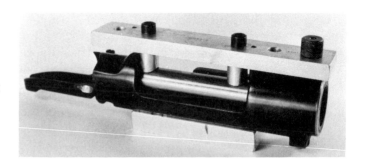

The simplest method of locating and boring holes is to utilize a jig such as this one by the B-Square Company. This locates the holes exactly to match the mounting holes of scope or sight base mounts.

problems. However, you can usually solve them with a little patience, strong words, and the use of the proper tools.

Let's start with a hardened receiver and go through the steps in mounting scope blocks. If you learn to do the job on such a gun, you won't have any trouble on the softer metals. If you have a sight-mounting jig from the B-Square Company you have many of the problems solved. You merely mount the top jig bar, the bore-aligning arbor, and the bottom bar in place on the receiver. The jig can be used on a barreled or unbarreled action. When installed correctly, it automatically locates the holes exactly to match the mount recoil shoulder, spaces the holes to match the mounting holes, positions the holes vertically on the centerline of the receiver, and aligns the holes with the rifle-bore centerline axis.

Place both the jig and receiver on the drill-press table. Although it's not necessary, you may wish to clamp solidly to the table with a drill-press vise. Almost all sight threads are 6×48 and the holes are drilled with a No. 31 bit which fits the tap threads properly. Although carbon-steel bits can be used, I prefer the high-speed-steel drill bits because they will run a bit faster without breaking as often. The proper speed for a No. 31 high-speed-steel drill bit is from 1600 to 1900 rpm; however, unless you have a pretty sophisticated machine you'll have to guess at the speed. The drill must be kept lubricated while drilling the holes with a drill lubricant or turpentine. When drilling blind holes, make sure you know the proper depth to drill. You don't want to bore through the barrel. Use a depth gauge to be sure you bore only deep enough for the screw. A depth-measuring caliper can be used for the measurement.

If you don't have a jig to accurately position the screw holes as well as guide the drill bit, you can

If you don't have a jig, remove the barreled action from the stock and place it in a good padded vise. Level rifle action, then level sight base in both directions with a cross test level. Clamp securely with parallel jaw clamps. Using a drill of smaller than tap size for mount, mark the location of the screw holes. Then remove the base from the action and clamp the action in a good drill-press vise, and drll for sight-base screws using a No. 31 high-speed drill bit.

still install sight or mounts, but the job becomes a bit trickier. *Regardless, make sure you locate all holes so the sight base won't get in the way of the bolt handle when in operation.*

The first step is to remove the action from the stock and remove the bolt if the gun is a bolt-ac-

If receiver is extremely hard, use a small hand grinder to grind away a bit of the surface where the holes will be drilled. Then use the tip of an acetylene torch to spot-anneal the screw-hole area. It should be heated to a deep blue, then allowed to cool slowly.

tion. Place the receiver in a padded vise and level it both lengthwise and crosswise. Use a small cross-test level for this job.

Position the mount or base on the receiver and clamp it in position with a parallel-jaw clamp. Level in position, then tighten down the clamp to hold the base securely in place. Choose a wire-drill size that will fit down in the base-screw hole without marring the threads. It should be so loose that it wobbles. Then place the clamped action and sight base in a drill-press vise and carefully spot-drill the hole. You should just mark the exact spot, not drill entirely through. Then remove the clamp and sight base and drill to the proper depth with the No. 31 drill.

If the receiver is case-hardened, it will have to be spot-annealed before it can be drilled and tapped. There are two methods of doing this, depending on what equipment you have. First a small stone is used to grind away a bit of the surface hardening. Then a small tip on an acetylene torch can be used to spot-anneal the area of the screw hole.

The area heated should be no larger than 5/16 inch directly in the location of the hole. The torch should be used to heat the area to a deep blue. Then allow to cool slowly. You can use a bit of heat-control paste to help control the heat in the area. Make sure you don't heat the area to a cherry red, or you'll harden the entire area so much it can't be drilled or tapped.

An easier way for the beginner is to use a large 2-to-3-pound soldering copper. Again grind down the area a bit, and drop a bit of noncorrosive sol-

If you don't have a tapping jig, chuck a 6×48 tap in the drill press and tap the hole by turning the drill-press chuck by hand. Then clean out oil and debris and install sight bases.

dering paste on the area. Apply a fairly large drop of solder directly over the hole location. Then, using a torch, heat the soldering iron to a good red heat. It should melt solder instantly. Place the soldering copper down on the drop of solder and hold it in place until the solder just begins to solidify. Quickly remove the soldering copper and wipe away the solder with a soft cloth before it becomes solid.

Once the holes have been bored you're ready to tap for the screws. The tap used is a 6×48, which is a special tap available in gunsmithing supply houses. Although taps are available in plug, bottoming, and taper styles, the tap most ordinarily used is the plug tap. It should be a carbon-steel tap instead of a high-speed-steel tap. If a high-speed-steel tap breaks off in a hole it is much harder to remove than a carbon-steel tap. To remove a carbon-steel tap you can either shatter it with a punch (if in an open hole) or drill it out if in a blind hole. Although some gunsmiths say that they have good luck with them, I've never been able to get tap extractors to work in this situation.

The tap should be held in a tapping jig such as the one sold by the B-Square Company, or you can place the tap in the drill-press chuck and turn it by hand. The tap should be lubricated with a good tap lubricant, or lard or white lead. Turn the tap in slowly, backing it out every quarter-turn to clean the chips away. If tapping a blind hole, remove the tap completely about every half-turn to clean the chip from the bottom of the hole. Drilling and tapping receivers for sight bases is not a particularly hard job, but it does take a certain feel, and if you've never done any of this type of machine-shop work, it would be a good idea to practice on some pieces of scrap steel before you start on a gun.

DOVETAIL SIGHTS

One problem may be a loosened dovetail sight. To determine if the sight is loose, clamp the gun barrel in a vise and mark with a very sharp pencil the location of the sight. Give it a sharp rap with a rawhide hammer (not a metal-faced hammer). If it moves, it needs to be tightened in the dovetail. You can remove the sight and peen down the edges of the dovetail cut a bit, or better yet, centerpunch the bottom of the dovetail cut. Both will tighten the sight when it is driven back in place.

Old dovetail sights may be removed by simply driving them, out using a soft copper punch and a lightweight ball-peen hammer. The dovetail sights are always driven out from left to right. New ones are driven in place from right to left, clamping the barrel in a vise with padded jaws.

If sight is loose in dovetail you can often tighten it in place by either peening down the edges of the dovetail just a bit, or lightly punching the bottom of the dovetail to roughen it.

Four different types of sight blades that are available. They're also available in different heights.

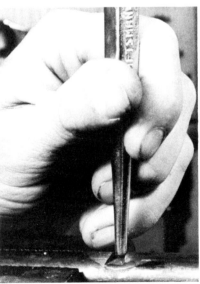

A sweat-on fully adjustable sight blade by the Williams Gun Sight Company. Installation of these sights can do a great deal to improve the accuracy of a gun.

You may prefer an aperture or peep sight instead of an open blade sight.

Cutting a New Dovetail

Although this seems to be a job for a machinist, with a little care and the proper tools you can cut a dovetail—for instance, in a shortened barrel—using nothing more than a hacksaw and a revamped triangular file.

Grind all the teeth off one side of the file. This provides a file that can be used to widen the dovetail without cutting the bottom, etc. You will also have to use a depth micrometer to determine proper depth. A dovetail should be cut to a depth of .090 inch.

The first step is to place the barrel in a padded vise and level it. Locate the dovetail and mark the location with a fine scribe. Then make the initial cuts with a new fine-toothed blade in a hacksaw. Don't make the cuts to full depth. Use the ground-down file to shape the dovetail, remembering that it must taper slightly. This is merely a matter of trial and error to determine fit, etc. The hardest part is making sure that the dovetail is perfectly parallel with the top of the barrel.

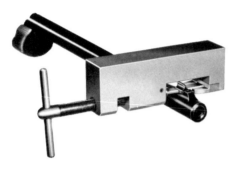

Installation of the front sights in the ramp is easy with this special tool which merely pushes the sight in or out of the dovetail. Cap with small hole is fitted over end of scope. Then the measuring square is fitted over the top of the scope to determine the exact center of bore. By sighting through scope at the grid you can determine whether the scope should be raised or lowered or if windage adjustments must be made.

INSTALLING FRONT RAMP SIGHTS

Sweat-on installation of front ramp sights has already been discussed in the chapter on metalworking. However, you will also occasionally come across ramp sights with screw holes for fastening the ramp in place with screws. In most cases this will mean boring and tapping a hole in the rifle barrel for the screw hole. The hardest part of the chore is getting the hole located top dead center of the barrel so the ramp will be installed parallel to the barrel. There are small jigs on the market that can make this job much easier, but it can also be done with a V-block setup and careful eyeballing before the hole is drilled. Make sure you set depth of the drill carefully so you don't drill through into the bore of the barrel.

PRESIGHTING

Once a scope has been mounted it should be presighted or "bore-sighted" before taken afield or to the range for final sighting in. For a bolt-action rifle the old-timers merely placed the rifle in position on a sandbag so that the bull was in the center of the bore. Then they adjusted the scope to suit. A much better method and one that's almost necessary for lever-action and other rifles is to use some sort of bore-sighting aid. There are several on the market, and two of my favorites are the Tasco model, which is a very economical "mechanical" sighting aid, and the Bushnell, which is an optical sighting aid. The Tasco model will do a great job, but takes a bit of practice. The Bushnell unit, on the other hand, costs quite a bit more but is much easier to operate. Either one would be one of the best investments a rifle shooter can make.

They can't be beat for last-minute sighting at a hunting camp to ensure that the gun hasn't been knocked out of whack during transit. In fact, nothing irritates me more than the sound of rifle fire coming from all sides of me hours before hunting season is to open. Several times while bowhunting deer (in Missouri the season is before the gun season) I have observed deer the evening hours before opening day when a barrage of shots could be heard all around. By opening day they were already spooky. In the Ozarks where I live you never know whether it's some joker getting in a last-min-

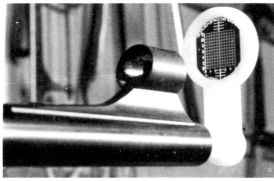

To presight or bore-sight a rifle with the Tasco scope guide, the grid post is first inserted in the gun muzzle.

ute sighting in, or a meat-collecting native getting his before the horde descends. In any case a good bore-sighting tool and the necessary screwdrivers can be mighty valuable instruments on a long-planned hunting trip.

To use the Tasco unit, mount the rifle on a bench rest, or sandbags, directing the rifle toward strong daylight, not the sun (or you might not be able to hunt again). The first step is to insert the scope guide into the muzzle of the unloaded rifle. Place the proper-size aperture cap over the objective bell of the scope. With the breech open, place the small arm of the "L-scale" on top of the scope, with the scale markings against the open breech. Note the numbered line which corresponds with the center of your rifle's bore. On centerfire rifles the firing pin will be at center; on rimfire rifles the extractor will be at center.

Look through the scope and rotate the front stanchion of the scope guide until the vertical centerline of the target pattern is parallel with the vertical line of the scope. Adjust the windage knob to bring the vertical wire of the scope in register with the centerline of the scope guide. Then adjust the elevation screw to match the scope's horizontal wire with the numbered line on the scope guide as indicated from the scale reading. Now with rifle bore sighted you're ready to go to the range for final sighting.

BORE SIGHTING WITH A COLLIMATOR

This is the best and easiest way of bore sighting. This device fits on the muzzle of the gun and emits an image of rays which are parallel with the bore. By aligning the reticle of the scope with the reticle of the collimator, then adjusting the elevation, you can quickly and easily bore-sight a gun in a minute or two. Then in most cases you will also need to bring the elevation dial on the scope up just a bit, which provides for the drop of the bullet in 100 yards.

SIGHTING IN

Once the rifle has been initially bore-sighted you're ready for sighting-in in the field or at the range. If in the field, use a large cardboard box to hold the target, taping in place. Use a sandbag or rolled-up

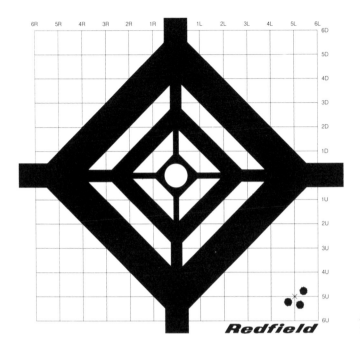

A Redfield sight-in chart and a typical three-shot group.

SIGHT-IN INSTRUCTIONS

1. Your rifle should be fired from a solid bench rest with the forearm, not the barrel, resting on a pad.

2. Sight-in at 25 yards for centerfire rifles and 15 yards for .22 rimfire. A shot striking the target zero at these ranges will put the bullet strike approximately 1 inch high at 100 yards.

3. Fire three carefully held shots using the corners of the diamond to maintain a constant sighting position. Locate the center of these shots on the grid pattern to determine direction and amount of correction required. See example in lower right hand corner of target. The center of this group is 5U-5L. Movement is required of 5 minutes of angle UP and 5 minutes of angle LEFT.

4. Scope graduations are usually ½ minute of angle or 1 minute angle (1 minute of angle = 1 inch at 100 yards). For 25 yard range adjustment must be 4 times amount shown on grid. In a scope having 1 MOA of adjustment graduation you would have to move 20 graduations left and 20 graduations up to bring the sample three shot group to the center of the target. The scope adjusting screws are marked showing direction of bullet strike change.

5. Fire your second three shot group after making the sight corrections required. This group should be in the center of the target.

6. After sighting in at 25 yards on the center of the target, then go to 100 yards for final zeroing. For centerfire rifles a shot group 1-2 inches high at 100 yards will yield shots approximately zero at 200 yards and 7-9 inches low at 300 yards.

blanket to hold the rifle in place, allowing the fore-end, not the rifle barrel, to rest on the steady rest. A blanket spread out on the ground will make you a bit more comfortable. Placing a heavy padded blanket between the gun butt and your shoulder will also help prevent flinching from the recoil. *Make sure you have a good solid backstop such as a soil bank.*

Sight in at 25 yards for centerfire rifles, and 15 yards for .22 rifles. When the bullet hits target bull at this range, it will place the bullet approximately 1 inch high when shot at 100 yards. Fire a three-shot group, carefully holding the gun steady and in position.

Use of a special scope-sight-in target will help a great deal because it is squared. An ordinary bull can also be used if you place 1-inch squares on the face. Then find the center of the group and adjust elevation and windage to suit. For instance, to correct the group on the Redfield chart shown you would raise the elevation adjustment 5 inches and move windage adjustment 5 inches to the left. Use the manual that comes with your particular scope to determine the graduations that are needed for the adjustment.

Allow the gun to cool, then fire another three-shot group and readjust again as necessary. You may wish to then fire a group at 100 yards.

A shotgun can also be fitted with a more accurate sight for use with slugs. Shown is a Model 1100 Remington with a Williams shotgun aperture sight.

SHOTGUN SIGHTS

When most of us think of sights we seem to forget about shotgun sights. But even though you may swear up and down you don't use those tiny little beads on the rib of your gun, try shooting an old gun without the bead sights and you'll find the difference. The sights give a quick reference, more in relation to where the gun is than as an actual sighting of the target, and when a shotgun is fitted with two sights you can also prevent canting or twisting a barrel such as a double-barrel gun during shooting. Installing a new sight bead is quite simple. If the old bead is missing, use a tiny burr grinder in a hand-held grinder to remove the metal screw from the threads. Run a tap of the proper size down the threads to make sure they're sharp and not filled (to determine the proper tap size, use different taps, hand-turned). Then simply screw in a new bead. There are specialized tools on the market that make this job a one-minute operation.

Use a drop of Loctite to hold new bead in place.

CHAPTER SEVEN

CARE AND REPAIR OF HANDGUNS

Handgunning is a hobby unto itself. Some handguns are the easiest of guns to work on, while others can quite frankly put you into a strait-jacket. There have been hundreds of articles and even books written on accurizing handguns, which is pretty much an individual project depending on the gun. Adding newer, better sights and honing the mechanism so the gun will have a smoother trigger pull and action are the most common techniques used for accurizing.

Of the three types of handguns—single-shot, revolver, and automatic—the revolver is probably most worked on. Today, however, there are probably more automatics than revolvers owned by handgun buffs.

One thing that should be remembered in working on handguns is to watch out for the Saturday-night specials. These were mass-produced, cheap, mail-order guns that quite literally should be cut apart and buried. More than one has blown up in a shooter's face, or the barrel has been shot off along with a bullet because of poor pinning, misalignment of cylinder and barrel, etc.

On the other hand, brand-name, quality handguns are fine works of the gunsmith's art and can be a joy to shoot and own, as well as to tinker with.

On older good-quality guns, the problem is usually nothing but old age. They become loose as parts become worn; the cylinder won't line up or turn properly, etc. Sometimes these guns can be

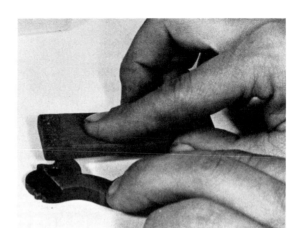

If the gun shoots hard, a bit of judicious stoning of the parts will help. Don't change the shape, merely remove the rough machining marks.

put back into practical use, other times they can't, depending on the gun and the problem. Remember, don't repair any gun unless you feel that it will be safe to fire. The job of tightening a loose revolver or automatic is a job for a pro. One thing that shouldn't be done is retightening by hammering. Although this is often suggested, you must be a fairly competent handgun man before you learn just where to hit and how hard without damaging a crane, etc. However, there are many jobs the beginning gun worker can tackle other than those listed under general gun work such as new stocks, bluing, etc.

SINGLE-SHOT GUNS

The old-time .22 single-shot pistols should be relegated to the wall, or have a competent gunsmith check them over before you tackle them. Although many were fine guns, their general looseness makes them dangerous. If you can find an old solid one, you'll be lucky. These guns are simple enough that you can normally figure out any type of problem without too much effort. One of the most common problems is an extractor that fails to work. This is normally due to excess oil or dirt around the extractor slot. Clean thoroughly and relubricate. Don't confuse the old-time single-shots with the new Thompson/Center Contender, which is a very fine gun.

REVOLVERS

Because of the number of moving parts, revolvers can have a great many things go wrong with them.

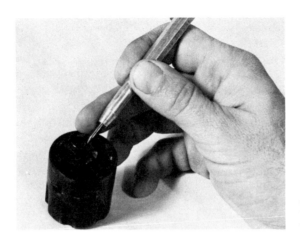

A malformed cylinder ratchet may be the problem. Usually this means buying a new cylinder.

The most you can do in most cases is replace older worn parts with new ones. In the case of the quality guns such as Smith & Wesson, merely removing the sideplates by turning out a few screws will give you an idea of the working mechanism. After examining closely, you can usually determine the problem. As a rule, single-action guns are a bit easier to work on than double-action guns. Here are a few things to look for and how to correct them.

Cylinder Doesn't Lock
This is normally caused by a broken bolt spring. Replace with a new spring.

Cylinder Play
On older models the cylinder will sometimes have a great deal of play, particularly from end to end. This often is caused by wear on the end of the tube or base-pin bushing which fits through the cylinder. Replace with a new base pin.

Worn Cylinder Ratchet
This takes a professional to rebuild. Best bet is to replace with a new cylinder.

Broken Handspring
A broken handspring is often indicated by a cylinder that won't turn when the gun is held straight up and cocked, but will when the gun is held down.

Broken Firing Pin
This is a common problem and quite simple to remedy, especially on single-action Colt-type guns, where the pins are held in place by a pin through

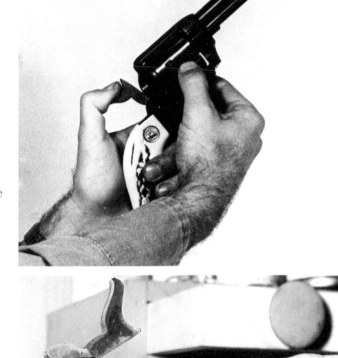

To test for a broken handspring, make sure gun is unloaded, then cock it and hold it down. Turn the cylinder. Then hold the gun pointed up and turn the cylinder. If it won't turn when held in the upright position, the handspring is broken.

To replace a broken firing pin on most single-action guns, drive out the holding pin on the back of the frame or the hammer. Then remove the firing pin and replace with a new one.

the hammer. Drive out the pin, then drive out the firing pin and replace it with a new one.

Timing

On double-action models the most common ailment is timing. Or rather when the hammer is cocked, the cylinder won't come into position or won't lock in position. To check for timing, slowly cock the hammer with your thumb until the trigger catches the hammer. While holding the hammer back in full-cock position, check the cylinder and attempt to turn it back counterclockwise. If the

Timing may be a problem on older guns. Slowly work the action of the unloaded gun and determine if the cylinder comes correctly in position with each turn.

cylinder is locked properly in place, it won't turn. However, if it moves, it is out of time. There may be any number of things causing the problem—the cylinder bolt may be loose or worn, the ratchet may be worn down, etc.

SEMI-AUTOMATIC PISTOLS

These guns have their own peculiar problems, the most common of which is feeding. This is usually the fault of the magazine instead of the gun. Examine carefully to make sure there are no dents or nicks in the magazine edges. A burred extractor may also catch the cartridge before it can rise up in place.

Doesn't Eject
This is a case for a thorough cleaning. However, the lip on the extractor may be damaged as well as the ejector. A recoil spring may also be too strong for the cartridge.

Doesn't Fire Full Magazine
In many cases this means the magazine spring is too weak.

Doesn't Extract
This suggests a roughened chamber or a broken extractor.

Doesn't Chamber
Often the magazine hasn't been placed in the pis-

MALFORMED
MAGAZINE LIP

Most semi-automatic pistol problems can be traced to a problem with the magazine rather than the pistol. A burred or dented magazine can prevent proper feeding resulting in other problems.

tol correctly and is either seated improperly in the frame or the feed ramp is in the way of the extractor.

Won't Close Completely
Normally dirt or debris prevents the slide from moving into position. However, occasionally a slide will become dented, causing exactly the same problem.

CHAPTER EIGHT

CARE AND REPAIR OF RIFLES

Many rifles are quite easy to work on, while others can be a real problem, such as the Remington fiberglass-stocked rifles. With these rifles the action is held in the receiver shell with pins and springs, and when you remove the receiver shell you'd better know where to look for the pins and springs or you may end up with a paper bag full of parts. On the other hand, such old favorites as the single-shot and pump rifles can provide a great deal of fun and interest to the beginning gun worker, and the ever-favorite bolt-action has been customized and rebuilt for years.

More home gun workers tinker with rifles, especially bolt-action rifles, than any other kind of gun. This is partly because of the accessibility in the past of economical bolt-action military rifles which could be converted to sporters, as well as the ease in working with these types of guns. Merely removing the guard screws on most models allows you to remove the entire barrel and receiver assembly for access to it or to the interior of the gunstock.

BOLT-ACTION RIFLES

Because this is the gun most often worked on, we will start with it. Many of the jobs mentioned for bolt-actions can also be done on other rifles, such as lever-actions.

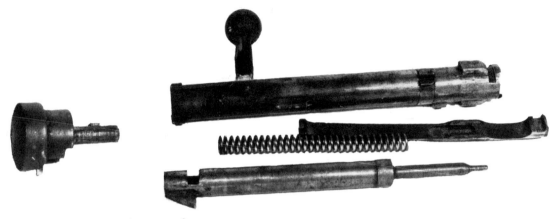

A typical military-style centerfire
bolt disassembled.

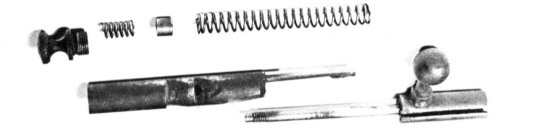

A typical .22 bolt disassembled.

One of the reasons the bolt-action is so popular
is the simplicity with which it is disassembled. To
remove the bolt on most guns you turn it up and
pull back, at the same time either pulling the trigger or releasing a catch on the left-hand side of the
receiver. On later-model bolt-actions, removing
the bolt is often done by pressing a small button or
lever on the left-hand side after flipping the safety
to the off position.

Taking a bolt apart for working on such things
as firing pins is just as easy, particularly on the
larger-caliber and military-style models. In most
cases this is done by cocking the gun first. Put the
safety to the on position, then unscrew the cocking
piece. Turn off the cocking knob. This allows you
to get to the firing pin and the firing-pin spring. In
most cases you can remove the extractor by turning it around the bolt until it can be disengaged.
Then push it off the T-shaped clip. When replacing
an extractor, make sure you don't bend it or damage the T-shaped clip. Sometimes you may have
to pry up the edge of the extractor a bit to get it to
flip over the edge of the bolt.

The bolts on .22 rimfire rifles generally are held

together in one of two ways. The first is by a set of pins. The second utilizes a screw-in cocking knob very similar to the heavier-style military bolt. The latter can be disassembled in the same manner as military-style bolts. These types often have two small springs that hold the pin and the cocking knob in place.

Trigger Adjustment

One of the most common improvements an amateur gun worker will make on his bolt-action is to adjust the trigger. In the case of an older-model military rifle that has been converted to a sporter, this may mean replacing the trigger mechanism. Military rifles such as the Enfield, Springfield, and Mauser utilize a take-up or double-pull trigger which has a camming action. This is a built-in safety factor with these types of guns, and although adjusting the trigger was at one time one of the first things that was done to a sporter, it's mighty dangerous and may cause accidental discharge. These triggers can, however, be made adjustable by a professional gunsmith. The best method is to use one of the manufactured adjustable trigger mechanisms made for that particular type of gun. In most cases these units, which are fully adjustable, can be fitted to your gun with just a little metalwork and a bit of inletting.

Making New Firing Pins

Often firing pins on older rifles will break, and as a rule you can't find a replacement. A piece of drill rod of the proper size makes an excellent firing pin. There is an easy method of turning down the end. Chuck the drill rod in a portable electric drill, then place the drill in a vise and turn it on. Using small files, shape the end of the drill rod to match the old firing pin. Make sure you leave plenty of radius between the tip of the pin and the body. If you make it square, it will break at that point. Once you have the end of the pin shaped correctly, you can then cut the drill-rod pin to the correct length and file in the notches needed. If the material you get is too soft and needs to be heat-treated, first heat the tip to a red color. Quench in oil and polish. Heat again until light blue, then quench again and polish.

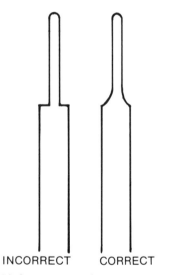

INCORRECT   CORRECT

Making a new firing pin may be required in some cases. Note shoulder must be rounded.

Tightening Trigger Guards

Make sure you keep the trigger guard tight on mil-

If a bolt works hard it can often be made to work easier by a light stoning of the surface with a fine Arkansas stone.

itary-style guns such as the Springfield or Mauser. If allowed to become loose it can effect the accuracy of these guns, as well as cause problems in magazine feeding. If the trigger guard is tight, but not seated properly in its place and at an angle, it may also cause feeding problems. The answer is to remove it, clean out the recess, then seat it properly, using a small rawhide hammer, and tighten in place.

Smoothing Bolt Operation

Difficult bolt operation is often caused by burrs on the cocking piece or the camming surfaces of the bolt. A very light stoning with a fine Arkansas stone will help a great deal in most cases. Or an extractor collar may be too tight, or hung up due to dirt or debris. Clean thoroughly, then use a bit of dry lubricant. Or you can place the bolt in a vise, holding it by the collar. Then place a wooden dowel that will fit fairly tightly down in the hole in the bolt from which the pin comes. Chuck the wooden dowel in an electric drill. Place a bit of graphite grease between the collar and the bolt and turn the bolt with the drill to "lap out" the bolt and collar assembly a bit.

Correcting Faulty Extraction in .22s

Regardless of whether the gun is a bolt-action, pump-action, or whatever, the main cause of poor extraction in .22 rifles is often a chamber that has been corroded through the use of too many .22 Short cartridges. The problem is a ring of corrosion formed just at the end of the short cartridge case. When a longer cartridge is placed in the chamber and fired, it expands into the corrosion and can't be extracted easily. This is a problem for the pro

as the gun will normally need a new barrel or a new "sleeve."

Lever-action rifles are the hardest for the amateur gun worker to work on because most of the action is hidden and inaccessible.

LEVER-ACTION RIFLES

These are the hardest rifles for most beginners to work on. Many of the parts aren't accessible to view, so you have to guess how they work and where they're located. Removing the stock on some guns will allow a better view of many of the parts.

To remove the trigger guard, note whether it is held in place by a screw or pin, then remove the screw or pin and remove the guard. Note whether the guard must be pulled straight up or pulled out toward the back a bit. Don't use force or you may cause damage.

To remove the bolt you must first drive out the pin that holds the bolt to the lever. This pin is normally located so it can be driven out from either side of the gun. Note the relative position of the lever top and the bolt so you can be sure you have the proper pin.

Fixing Jams
Jamming is normally the result of a cartridge guide becoming loose. The solution is to tighten up the screw that holds the guide in place.

Smoothing Action
A lever-action rifle utilizes a lot of moving parts, particularly camming parts, and a good stoning with a fine Arkansas stone will help smooth up these parts a great deal. Remember, however, that a little will go a long way with this operation. You don't want to change the size and shape of any of

the parts but merely remove any roughness left by the initial machining of the parts.

Fixing Extractor or Ejector

With a lever-action these parts are fairly easy to see, and a simple examination while working the gun slowly will normally give an indication of the problem.

Trigger Adjustment

As a rule, trigger assemblies on lever-action rifles are not easily adjustable. One thing that should be remembered with these guns is that they can accidentally fire even though the safety is on, because the safety doesn't lock the bolt solidly in place as it does on a bolt-action rifle.

AUTOLOADING GUNS

Like their shotgun and pistol counterparts, semi-automatic rifles are an entirely different ball game. Normally about the only way you can determine how an autoloader is working is to test-fire it, using at least three cartridges in the magazine. Probably the most common problems of an autoloading gun are failure to feed, extract, or reject, and any one of these problems can be caused by one simple thing: a roughened or corroded chamber. Although some gun writers recommend stoning an autoloader to get more smoothness from the parts, for the amateur this can easily botch up a good gun, because the stoning process is quite tricky. You might end up with a gun that doesn't cycle properly at all.

Trigger assemblies on semi-automatic rifles are also not readily adjustable. Occasionally check the safety of the trigger hammer to make sure there is no wear or play in it there. If there is, take the gun to a competent gunsmith and allow him to do the work needed.

PUMP-ACTION RIFLES

A common problem is failure to feed, caused by a dented magazine tube. This can also be caused by poorly reloaded ammunition, so check with new ammunition before attempting to peen out the dents. On some guns, particularly some of the older .22s, the magazine metal is so soft you have to be really delicate with the hammer.

To check the action on rifles such as pumps and automatics you will need dummy cartridges. These can often be purchased from sporting-goods stores, but you'll probably have to order them.

After cocking the hammer, try to pull back on the fore-end or cocking piece. If the fore-end retracts it means the breech bolt is not locked properly. This is often caused by worn parts or dirt.

Repairing a Dented Magazine

A dented magazine can often cause cartridges to stick rather than to feed up into the gun. The solution is to hammer out the dent, using a small brass hammer and an inside follower, made of drill rod to suit the inside of the magazine. Then note if cartridges will slide in magazine properly.

A common problem with pump guns is a dent in the magazine tube which prevents them from feeding. Peen out lightly with brass hammer and metal rod follower.

One common problem with single-shot rifles is an extractor which fails to hook the cartridge because of dirt behind it.

SINGLE-SHOT RIFLES

Single-shot rifles, like single-shot shotguns and pistols, are quite simple; they can be examined closely to determine most problems and disassembled quite easily. The main problem is that you may not be able to get parts and may have to make any that are worn or missing.

Regardless of what type of gun, the problem most often encountered is bad extraction of the fired cartridge. This can be caused by many things, but the most common is that the extractor itself may not be working because of a malformed hook, or even dirt or grease in the bolt face, preventing the extractor from properly "hooking" the rim of the cartridge.

CHAPTER NINE

CARE AND REPAIR OF SHOTGUNS

I guess you could say I'm a shotgun man. I love to collect, shoot, and work on shotguns, particularly older doubles. A beginning gun worker can do a lot of repair work on most shotguns because the guns themselves are quite simple.

CUSTOM-FITTING YOUR SHOTGUN

The most important thing with a shotgun is that it fit the shooter properly. Have you ever bought a new shotgun and found you couldn't hit the proverbial barn with it? Or perhaps you've inherited a handed-down family gun and in no way can score a hit. In either case, don't blame yourself too fast—the gun probably doesn't fit you.

In comparison to a rifle, a shotgun has no rear sight; the shooter's eyes substitute for the rear sight. The front "bead" and shooter's eyes line up the target. For consistent accuracy, a shotgun must "fit" the individual so that his eyes are properly aligned with the barrel and the front bead or sight. The gun should come up easily without hanging up on clothes. You should be able to bring it up into the pocket of your shoulder and upper arm each time without any conscious effort. In short, a shotgun should fit you like a pair of time-worn bluejeans. New guns are for people of average build, and most old guns have been fitted to a particular shooter, so a gun, old or new, should be fitted to you, the shooter.

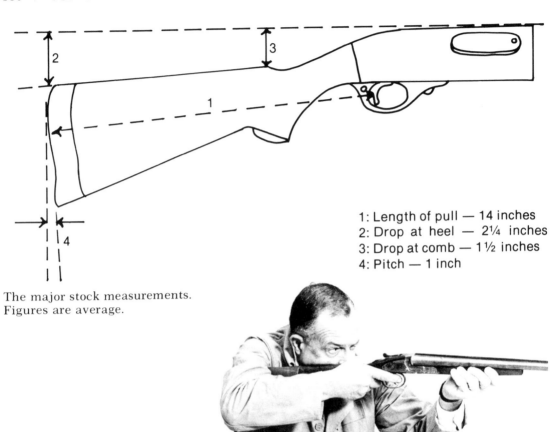

1: Length of pull — 14 inches
2: Drop at heel — 2¼ inches
3: Drop at comb — 1½ inches
4: Pitch — 1 inch

The major stock measurements. Figures are average.

In this instance stock is too short, and recoil will be pretty hard.

Several alterations can be made to a shotgun stock to make it fit you better. The typical stock measurements of a shotgun include length of pull, drop at comb, and pitch and drop at heel.

Let's take length of pull first, because it's the most commonly changed measurement. This is actually the measurement from the front of the trigger to the center of the back edge of the butt-plate or recoil pad. The correct length of pull is very important, because if it is too short, the gun will kick harder, since you don't get the butt correctly in place each time. By the same token, if the stock is too long, it will slide over to the muscle of your upper arm, and after about a half-dozen shots you'll be black and blue in that area.

Most new guns come from the factory with a 14-inch length of pull. This dimension is pretty well standard. For years, gunsmiths have related length

If stock is too long, butt has a tendency to slip off shoulder onto your upper arm. This is uncomfortable and will cause a bruise in a short time.

If comb is too low, or pitch too much, the shooter has to drop his head uncomfortably low to maintain sight picture.

of pull to the height of the individual as follows: up to 5'6", length of pull 13½ inches; from 5'7" to 6', length of pull 14 inches; over 6', length of pull 14½ inches.

Although these are pretty standard measurements, depending on your body build, arm length, etc. you may have to adjust them as much as ¼ to ½ inch. You can readily change the length of pull by either cutting off the stock to decrease the length of pull, or by adding a recoil pad or spacers to increase the length of pull.

To determine the length of pull you need, place the butt of the gun in the crook of your arm and place your finger on the trigger. The first joint of your trigger finger should just fit over the center of the trigger. Many gunsmiths utilize a pull and drop gauge, which is nothing more than a specialized type of wood square. The one rule many forget

The time-tested method of measuring for length of pull is to place butt in crook of your elbow. The first joint of your first finger should just touch the middle of the trigger.

is to make sure you wear your hunting clothes when you take these measurements.

If you lived in Europe and had enough money, you could use a special "try gun" with movable parts which can be utilized to fit the stock to you perfectly, and then these measurements can be taken to build your custom-fitted stock. Reinhart Fajen, Inc., of Warsaw, Missouri, has a try stock for $200, or possibly you could rent one. You can, however, do an adequate job of making these measurements in your home shop, but it will naturally take a bit of time. For instance, if you have determined that the stock is a bit too short for you, remove the butt plate and make a ¼-inch plywood spacer to fit between the plate and stock. This doesn't have to be fancy—it is merely a measuring device. If you still need more length, add another ¼-inch spacer. Remember, on a gun without a recoil pad, you will add almost an inch with the recoil pad. If you still don't have enough length (which in most cases will be quite unusual), purchase one of the boot-type recoil pads and slip this over the stock as well. Plastic spacers and a recoil pad can then be used to lengthen the stock to suit.

If, on the other hand, the stock is too long, reverse the process, cutting off only ¼ inch at a time. Again you can cut off up to ¾ inch without any danger, because the length can be brought back to the same as it was with the addition of a recoil pad. When cutting off a stock, make sure you maintain the original pitch unless you want it changed.

Changing the Pitch

Pitch can be very important to the shooter and can make a great deal of difference in accuracy. One of the problems of adding a recoil pad with a flat back is that you will be changing the pitch of the gun a bit because a plastic buttplate normally has a curved protruding section at the toe of the plate. A trap recoil pad is shaped more like a buttplate, but doesn't provide much help to the average field shooter.

The average pitch on most shotguns is 1 inch. If your gun has too much pitch it will make you undershoot. If it has too little pitch it will make you overshoot. This is changed by merely changing the angle of the back of the butt of the gun stock. But it should be done carefully and only a little at a time, because a little goes a long way with this

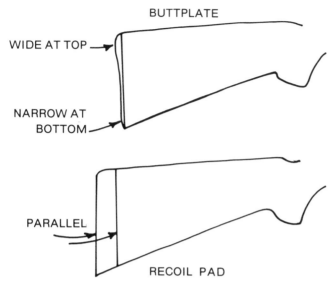

WIDE AT TOP →

BUTTPLATE

NARROW AT
BOTTOM →

PARALLEL →

RECOIL PAD

Pitch of gun is important
too—and a recoil pad will change
it.

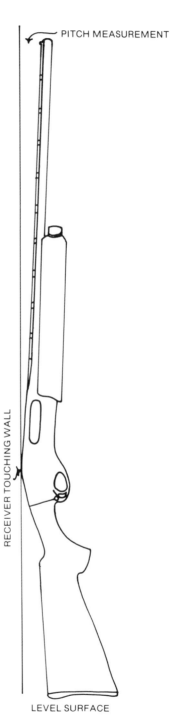

PITCH MEASUREMENT

RECEIVER TOUCHING WALL

LEVEL SURFACE

By standing in front of a mirror
and swinging gun naturally into
shooting position you can
determine whether gun fits.

The pitch is measured not at the
butt but at the muzzle, with the
gun against a wall as shown.

alteration. In fact, a ⅛-inch wedge spacer placed on either top or bottom between buttplate and stock can be used as a try fit before any material is cut from the stock.

Other differences lie in the individual shooter's neck length and positioning of the cheek on the gunstock. Everybody is different, and ideally the gun should fit perfectly, so you may have to change the drop at the heel or raise or lower the comb to find the perfect fit.

To check final fit of the gun, face a mirror in your natural shooting position with gun unloaded and pointed down. In a smooth easy motion, bring the gun straight up and pointing directly at itself in the mirror. You can quickly see if the barrel consistently comes up too high, too low, or off to one side or the other with this test. Again, make sure you wear your hunting clothes.

After determining the changes needed, alter the stock as needed. Incidentally, this is also an excellent time to improve on a weak finish or to refinish an older gunstock, but be careful to keep paint remover off the new recoil pad.

Installing a Recoil Pad

One of the simplest but most effective customizing jobs you can do to a shotgun is to add a recoil pad. As we discussed before, this may be necessary to lengthen a too-short stock, or you may wish to add the pad for comfort alone. A recoil pad will cut down on fatigue and flinching, and at the end of a day's shooting at clay pigeons, quail, or pheasants, you'll be mightily glad you added that little rubber bumper on the back of your favorite scattergun.

First step is to remove the buttplate from the shotgun. Measure the correct length of pull, utilizing a carpenter's square or pull and drop gauge. Assuming that the pitch is to remain the same, scribe a line lightly around the stock, parallel with the existing end and at the correct length. If the gunstock is finished, cover with masking tape up to the scribed line. This will prevent splinters from the sawing operation. Needless to say, the stock should be removed from the gun for ease of working. Cut the stock off, making sure you cut it square. This can be done on a bandsaw, with a thin shim to hold stock and action parallel to the table, or you can use a fine-toothed cabinetmaker's handsaw or even a new hacksaw. The cut end is

Measure for length of pull and mark line parallel with butt, using a metal scribe. Wrap tape around stock and cut stock to proper length. Make sure butt cut is square. Use disc or belt sander if possible.

then squared up by sanding on a disc sander or belt sander or by holding it in a vise and sanding it with a sanding block. Position the recoil pad on the stock and mark the rough shape of the stock, on the pad, leaving some excess. Then rough-grind the recoil pad to the shape of the cutoff line. Do not, however, grind down to the finish line at this time. Make sure you also keep the line at the toe of the stock correct. In fact, it's a good idea not to grind off any of the toe at this time.

Put the pad back on the stock and use an awl to mark for the screw holes. Bore with a small-size pilot bit, but not too deep. If the screw holes fall just to the side of one of the existing holes, plug them first with a wooden plug. Then put the recoil

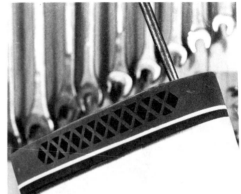

Mark rough outline on an extra-large pad and rough-cut it to shape on a disc sander or belt sander. Don't cut to line, and make sure you don't change line of stock at toe of pad. Place pad back in position on stock and mark screw locations through pad with an awl. After counterboring for screws, using bit about ¾ size of screw, place a bit of beeswax on each screw and turn it down through the recoil pad, then screw pad in place. Use two screwdrivers to fasten pad securely and squarely.

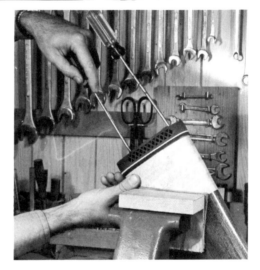

pad on the stock and fasten it in place with the screws supplied. Add spacers as needed. Some people like to add a bit of glue to help hold the pad, but this can be a real hassle when it comes time to remove the pad, and you obviously don't want to use glue if the gun is held together with a stock bolt. The screws should hold the recoil pad firmly in place without any crack showing. One of the secrets is to use two screwdrivers, and again make sure they fit the screw head perfectly. Clamp the stock in a padded vise, place the recoil pad in position, and then push the screws down through the pad, turning them with the screwdrivers until they both start to pull down the pad. Tighten the screws alternately a little at a time to keep the pressure equal. Using the two screwdrivers also prevents extra injury to the tiny X-holes cut in the back of the pad for screwdriver entry.

There are any number of ways of removing the

After final shaping is done on a disc sander, tape is removed and final sanding is done with extremely fine sandpaper.

excess portions of the pad. Some gun workers have even done it with rasps and hand sanding blocks. A disc sander just can't be beat for this job, but you can also use a belt sander clamped in your vise and hold the pad against it. Make sure you continue the lines of the stock when doing this job, and don't "bob" the toe or the top of the pad. When the recoil pad fits the gun correctly, use a finishing sander and fine sandpaper to remove any rough marks left by the coarse paper. Remove the tape and touch up any small nicks or marks you might have made on the stock, using a good oil stock finish rubbed on with your fingers, or a finish compatible to the finish on your stock. If you are careful and have the stock taped properly, you shouldn't have any refinishing problems to contend with.

Incidentally, fitting a recoil pad to a rifle is done in the same manner, as are basic stock alterations.

REMOVING DENTS

Probably one of the most common problems with all types of shotguns is a dent in the barrel. Although some shooters will be extremely picky about other things, they seem to ignore this problem—and it is a problem. Not only can the dent cause deformed pellets, which affects the pattern, but it can make a gun barrel blow up. About the only way you can effectively remove a dent from a gun barrel is to use tools made specifically for that purpose, and for that particular size bore. The

Dents in shotgun barrels can easily be removed with an expanding dent plug. The plug made for the specific gauge is expanded until it will fit tight under the dent. It is fitted in the barrel using a wooden dowel to punch it down from the chamber. Using a brass hammer, tap around the dent until it comes up or the plug becomes loose.

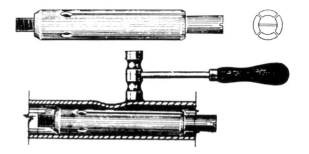

tool is a bit expensive, and unless you later plan to do a bit of "paying gunsmithing," the cost isn't warranted. This is one of those quite simple jobs that must be taken to a professional unless you wish to invest in the tools.

Another problem with removing dents is in knowing which ones can be removed easily, which will be hard, and which will be almost impossible. Dents that are near the breech end of the barrel are almost impossible for even the experts to remove because of the thickness of the metal. On the other hand, dents near the muzzle may cause a fracture of the barrel if too much force is used to bring the dent out of the thin metal.

You can purchase dent-removal tools which are merely expanding plugs. In use the plug is placed in the barrel and expanded until it fits snugly under the dent. A large wooden dowel is used to punch the plug down from the chamber into the barrel. Then a light brass hammer is used around the outside edge of the dent, much like automobile body work, to bring up the dent. If the plug becomes loosened before the dent is removed, merely expand it some more and continue light hammering and retightening until the dent is removed. If done properly, there won't be any need for rebluing the barrel. Make sure bore and tool are clean before using, or you may damage the inside of the barrel, or the tool. When finished, remove the dent remover from the breech instead of the muzzle or you may damage the choke of the gun.

Examine the bore carefully with a good light to make sure the dent has been raised properly from the inside. If it looks good from the outside but still shows from the inside, lap the barrel carefully, using the techniques and tools mentioned in the cleaning chapter. If a barrel has become bent it should be taken to a professional gunsmith. A shotgun which has a bulge should also be taken to a pro; you want to be sure removing the bulge won't make the gun unsafe to shoot.

CUTTING OFF A BARREL

If a shotgun barrel muzzle has been damaged or blown away, it can often be cut away, producing a shorter barrel. That is, if you can still have a barrel over the legal length of 18 inches. The job is not particularly hard, but will result in a true open-bore gun, unless you want to install an adjustable choke on the end of the gun. Although you can do the barrel-cutting work yourself, installation of the choking device should be left to the professionals. Many require the use of a metal lathe for attachment.

Think carefully before cutting off a barrel. If you must do it, use an ordinary pipe cutter to mark, not cut, the barrel. Tape under the cutter rollers will prevent marking the bluing. Then use a hacksaw with fine-tooth blade and carefully cut away the barrel end. Use crocus cloth to polish and smooth the muzzle.

To cut a barrel off, mark it first with a pipe cutter. Note tape prevents marring bluing. Then cut off with a fine-tooth hacksaw and smooth with crocus cloth.

SHOTGUN PATTERNS

A scattergun is only as good as its pattern, and to really shoot consistently you should pattern your gun, not only at different yardages, but using different types of shotshells. The standard method of patterning is to shoot from 40 yards at a piece of paper with a 30-inch circle on it. After shooting, count the number of shot holes found inside the circle, then divide this by the number of shot in

From this table you can determine the number of pellets in your test load.

TABLE OF SHOT SIZES

Size	9	8	7½	6	5	4	2	BB
	●	●	●	●	●	●	●	●
Diameter	.08	.09	.095	.11	.12	.13	.15	.18
Number of Shot to the Ounce (Average)	585	409	350	224	171	136	89	50

the charge. A full-choke gun should place up to 75% of the shot in the circle; a modified, 55% to 65%; an improved cylinder, 45% to 55%; a true cylinder, 35% to 45%. Now that you have determined how your gun patterns—whether it is a true full-choke, cylinder-bore, etc.—the next step is to shoot it at different distances to determine the changes you will have in your pattern. Most of us shoot at game closer than 40 yards, and patterning your gun at 20, 30, or even 15 yards may give some explanation as to why. It's also a good idea to shoot at several targets and look for consistent holes in the pattern. Some shooters also like to pattern with various types of loads to determine which works best for them.

Proper cleaning and lubrication of an automatic can prevent many of the problems with that type of gun such as jamming in cold weather. Use lubricant sparingly.

Adjusting the recoil can tune up an automatic.

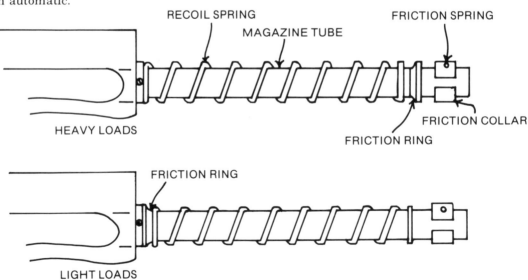

RECOIL SPRING
MAGAZINE TUBE
FRICTION SPRING
FRICTION COLLAR
FRICTION RING
HEAVY LOADS

FRICTION RING
LIGHT LOADS

REPAIRING INDIVIDUAL GUNS

Like all gunsmithing work, careful consideration must be given to the safety of the gun, particularly older guns which may be loose or unsafe and can literally explode in your face.

Autoloaders

One of the most common problems with automatic shotguns is jamming or misfiring in cold weather because of the use of improper gun oils or, more commonly, overuse of gun oils. If a gun is to be used in extremely cold weather, dismantle and clean it thoroughly with cleaner-degreaser. Then apply only a light touch of oil, or one of the dry gun lubricants.

One of the best tune-ups you can give an automatic shotgun is to adjust the recoil spring or gas cylinder for the types of load you will be using. Often a gun set for heavy loads won't function properly when used with light loads. Using light loads in a gun set for heavy loads not only causes more recoil, but may damage the gun mechanism as well.

To adjust, examine the gun to see if directions are printed on it, such as on the magazine tube under the fore-end, or contact the manufacturer for specific instructions on the adjustment procedure. Sometimes the recoil adjustment is by a friction ring, as on the Browning.

A broken or cracked fore-end on an autoloader should be replaced, as it functions as a portion of the action by holding the moving parts together. Burrs or nicks on a friction tube should be removed, but the tube should not be polished.

Almost all problems are caused by dirt and grease and debris. These are one of the most reliable types of guns and if kept clean and lubricated properly, they will usually perform for years without any problems. However, because of their complicated mechanism, any serious malfunctions should be corrected by a professional gunsmith.

Pumps

Pump-gun problems are normally quite simple to remedy. For instance, a feeding problem may be caused by a dented magazine tube. To remove dents, fit a hardwood dowel into the tube and use a small brass hammer to lightly peen out the dents, much in the same manner as you would correct a

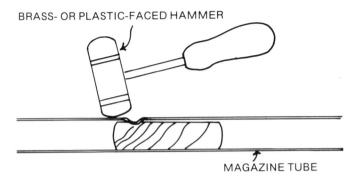

BRASS- OR PLASTIC-FACED HAMMER

MAGAZINE TUBE

One common problem with pump guns is dents in the magazine tube. Use a wooden dowel and small brass hammer to bring dents up.

dent in an automobile body. Peen around the outside of the dent with light blows so you don't crack or damage the tube.

If the gun fails to extract, one of the most common problems is a broken extractor or a jammed extractor spring which may be caused by dirt or grease. Remove the spring, clean the recess, and try again. If it's still a problem you may have to replace the spring.

The block in a takedown gun may sometimes become loose in the frame or receiver. To correct, move the bolt-adjustment bushing to tighten it. This is a sleeve which is fastened onto the barrel. The outside of it is threaded with an interrupted or sometimes half thread. The slide or lug is loosened to allow the sleeve to turn. Turn the sleeve in a couple of notches, then retighten it back in place. Try the barrel and receiver together. If still not tight, tighten a couple more notches.

Double- and Single-Barrel Shotguns

As a rule these are the most reliable and the easiest to work on, except for the spring mechanism on some guns such as the older Ithacas or Parkers. In fact, some of these older guns are becoming such collectors' items that you might wish to have a professional do any major repair work. For instance, one of the problems with older double barrel shotguns is that the barrel sometimes becomes so loose it won't lock securely down in the frame. Although this can be remedied a bit by peening the metal down around the standing breech, then filing until the barrel closes securely, in most cases the job should be taken to a professional so he can make absolutely sure you have a gun that will be safe to shoot.

One thing that makes it easier to work on these types of guns is that by removing the side or bottom

Removing side or bottom plates enables you to see the working mechanism of double-barrel guns.

plates you can normally examine the entire working mechanism quite easily. Side plates normally have a single long screw passing through both to hold them in place, and some may have smaller auxiliary screws in the front of the plate as well, or a tongue-shaped piece may help hold the front in place. The bottom plate is normally held in place by two or three screws. One of the screws will probably be under the head of the trigger guard, in which case you must remove the screw holding the trigger guard and swing the guard out of the way to get to the screw. In some cases you may have to take the guard off entirely. After you have loosened the screws, don't use a screwdriver to pry the plates from the frame. Instead use a rawhide hammer and tap the frame around the plate until it loosens.

Occasionally after disassembling a double-barrel gun, then reassembling it, the trigger may work a little hard or slow. This is because screws have been pulled down too tightly and parts are rubbing against each other. The remedy is to place a small metal shim so it will prevent the screws going from the trigger guard into the upper tang from being tightened too much.

Quite often you'll find a broken firing pin on an older double- or single-barrel shotgun. These are normally quite easily removed and replaced. Although you can make some of the pins easily, they can also be purchased through the gun manufacturers, or from gunsmith supply houses.

Another common problem is a loose fore-end. These can often be repaired by bending a weakened spring back in shape or replacing it with a new one.

CHAPTER TEN

CUSTOMIZING AND SPORTERIZING

To many gun owners the real fun of working on guns is in customizing, accurizing, or sporterizing them. This can run anywhere from the simple addition of sling swivels or new sights for accurizing a handgun to the complete revamping of a gun, such as making a sporter from a military rifle or making a boy's rifle from an economical .22.

CUSTOMIZING A .22

Let's start with a .22. This is one of the best methods for the beginning gun worker to acquire some practical experience. Economical .22s can be purchased brand new for around $35 to $40, and although the gun isn't worth a whole lot, it can be revamped to make it shoot better and fit better. And you don't have to worry about the initial gun being unsafe to shoot, as might be the case with an older "throwaway" gun. Working on a couple of these guns will give you an idea of what is involved and how to set up your work area, and may even teach you a few new words.

The first step in revamping these guns is to change sights. The front sight on most of these guns is a single-piece block affair that fits in the front dovetail. Often such a sight protrudes past the edge of the barrel and can snag on brush and weeds, making it a general nuisance. In addition, it often doesn't fit properly in the dovetail and can be moved quite easily, making it hard to keep the

A good learning experience for the beginning gun worker is to purchase an economical .22 bolt-action rifle and "customize" it a bit. The finished gun incorporates better sights and a sling, and has been cut down to suit a youngster.

gun accurate. Replace the sights with better adjustable sights. There are any number of sights that can be used for this purpose.

You might wish to install a scope. However, it would be defeating your purpose at this point, as you're using the rifle as a learning experience. You can install sights by sweat-on soldering, or learn to drill and tap, and if you ruin a blue job or botch up a stock you haven't lost much, but gained a

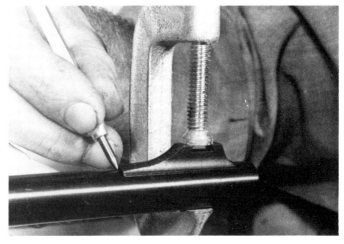

New front ramp is located and scribed around for soldering in place. Bluing is removed in area scribed, then ramp is soft-soldered in position.

great deal of experience. A simple sight that is more contoured and has a white, gold, or fluorescent bead for easier viewing may simply be driven back in place and used with a better buckhorn-style open sight that also utilizes a white "finding dot." Or you may prefer to utilize a ramp and sight combined with a receiver sight. This provides a bit more accurate sight for many people and provides an "extra" if the rifle is to be presented to a youngster for target shooting. Place the rifle barrel in a padded vise and drive out the front sight, driving it from left to right. Use a brass rod or punch so you don't mar the sight or surrounding metal.

If you're going to be installing a front ramp sight, there are two methods that you can utilize. The first is to drive a dovetail slot blank in the dovetail to fill it up, then solder the ramp to the gun. Or you can bore and tap for the ramp. An alternative is to use a Williams shorty ramp which has a small locking nut that slides in the dovetail. You merely

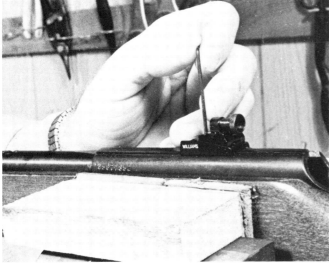

Cheap rear sights are driven out of dovetail and replaced with quality peep sight.

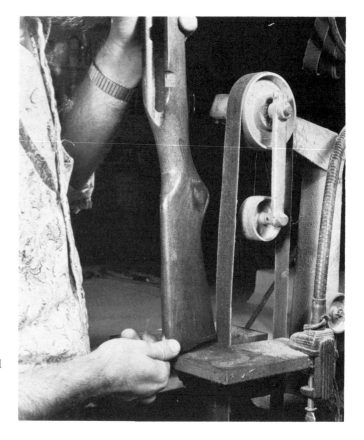

Remove buttplate from cut-off piece and install it on the squared up end of stock, then grind to fit stock. You may wish to tape the stock to prevent marring the finish.

drive this in place in the dovetail and place the sight over it, screwing the sight to the holding nut. On some guns, however, the dovetail may be so wide that it will show under the new ramp. In this case you would have to use the filler block.

The rear sight is driven out in same manner and replaced. Again, there are a number of sight combinations that can be utilized. A Williams Guide Receiver Sight with a standard aperture was used in this case. It is available with a dovetail base that will almost fit most .22s. A bit of careful filing on the sight bottom will help. This is driven in place from the right to the left. Incidentally, you might want to provide a hooded front sight if the youngster will be using the gun for target practice. The main thing is to make sure you match the front sight to the rear sight, or you may never be able to get the gun sighted in properly.

Choosing the right sights can be difficult. However, Brownell's, Williams, and other major sight manufacturers include tables in their catalogs that match their products with specific guns. You can send for these catalogs or study them at your local gun dealer's store.

If the .22 is to be used by a youngster you might also want to cut down the stock to fit. Using the old length-of-pull measurement from the crook of the elbow to the first joint of the first finger, determine the length of pull. Then measure this on the stock, and scribe a line parallel to the butt (not the buttplate). Cut off at this point, using a bandsaw or sharp handsaw or even using a hacksaw with a new blade.

Use a rasp or belt sander to smooth the butt and make sure it is square. Then remove the plastic buttplate from the cut-off piece of stock. Scribe a centerline down the center of the stock butt. Put the buttplate in place and mark for screw holes, making sure the buttplate protrudes on all sides—that is, that no wood sticks out past the buttplate. Then fasten the buttplate in place with the screws. The buttplate will now have to be ground down to fit the cut-off stock. This is best done on a belt or disc sander, although you can do it with a rasp and file.

In some cases you may also want to make the handgrip a bit smaller, especially if the youngster has a small hand.

Use cold bluing to touch up any spots you might have messed up installing the sights. Install sling swivels and you're in business. Take the rifle out and sight it in properly.

CONVERTING MILITARY RIFLES

Converting or sporterizing military rifles used to be a big thing with riflemen, mostly because of the availability of good military models at an economical price. Today, however, there aren't as many good ones to be found. If you just want a good bolt-action centerfire rifle your best bet is to purchase a factory model and then accurize it. You can, however, purchase actions, both barreled and un-barreled, trigger assemblies, barrels, stock blanks, etc., and literally build your own custom rifle. And there are still a few good military rifles available.

I show the sporterizing of a military rifle here because all the methods and techniques used in accurizing and customizing a factory model, and even some of the techniques for custom building a rifle, are needed for the job. The rifle is a 6.5 Italian Carcano. This is a relatively economical

One of the most popular gunsmithing projects is to convert a military rifle to a sporter. Shown here is an Italian Carcano 6.5 rifle. The converted rifle utilizes Williams sights and a Herter stock blank.

military rifle and one that is still frequently available at gun shops.

One of the reasons the gun is still available in quantities is that the receiver has a split bridge. In other words, the bolt must be drawn back through a slot in the back of the bridge to cock the gun. This makes it almost impossible to mount a scope on the gun without a lot of hassle. On the other hand, receiver sights can be installed without too much trouble.

Regardless of what type of gun you're sporterizing, the first step, if it's an older model, is to take it to a competent gunsmith and have him check it to make sure it will be safe to fire. This should especially be done on the headspacing.

Planning the Conversion

Okay, you've got a good bill of health on the old gun and you're ready to proceed. Sit down and decide exactly what you want to use the gun for and how you want to convert it—for instance, scope or iron sights, Mannlicher or sporter stock, standard or altered bolt, etc.

It's a good idea to get specific information on your particular type of gun. There are several good books out on sporterizing or converting specific guns. *The American Rifleman* magazine has several reprints out, such as "Remodeling the '03A3 Springfield," and there may be one for your gun. In addition, the Williams Gun Sight Company has excellent material on converting some of the more popular models. With the information in hand on your particular type of gun you're ready to order stock blank, scope, sights, trigger assemblies, and other parts. Get the appropriate catalogs and order the materials you will need.

Breaking Down the Gun

The first step in converting is to remove the old stock, then take off any excess metal parts that won't be needed for the converted rifle. For instance, the rear sights on the Italian rifle shown were situated on a solid block of metal that encircled the rifle barrel. This was removed by unscrewing a holding pin and tapping off. Save all these pieces. You don't know when you might need a piece of metal or a screw that just might work for one of these guns. Incidentally, one of these old stocks fitted with a ¾-inch wooden dowel makes a great "toy gun" for a youngster, so don't throw it away.

While you're waiting for the stock or other goodies to arrive you can smooth up or file down any rough areas and in general get the action and barrel ready to use.

Choosing and Rough-Cutting the Stock Blank

The rifle shown utilizes a stock blank from Herter's. If you have access to your own walnut you might want to cut your own blanks and cure them yourself for a really special gun, although it will take several years of barn or garage curing to get a stable blank.

The next step is to make sure the two sides of the blank are square with each other. Normally they will be if the blank is from a reputable company, but it's a good idea to check, using a small square. Then make a drawing of the stock you desire. If you can get a good sporter rifle to copy from, you're in business; however, you will probably have to alter the blank somewhat to suit your particular gun. Shown is a standard measurement for a sporter-style stock, as well as a squared drawing of the stock cut for the 6.5 rifle. A much faster way would be to order a semi-inletted blank from Reinhart Fajen, Herter's, or one of the other stock manufacturers. These are available for most military rifles and most of the work has been done for you.

If you're using a blank the next step is to rough-

The wood blank used to build the stock.

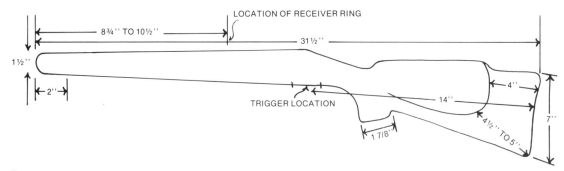

Dimensions of a typical Mauser-style sporter stock.

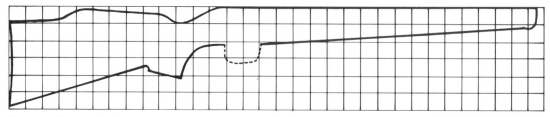

Pattern for stock shown on 6.5 rifle. Each square equals 1 inch.

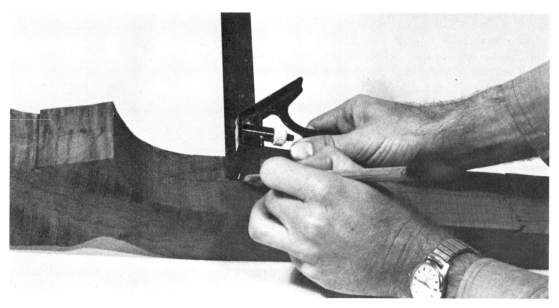

After cutting blank to rough outline on bandsaw, scribe line completely around blank, oversetting it ½ to ¾ inch to right side to allow for cheekpiece.

cut the outline of the stock on a bandsaw. Then mark a centerline around the entire stock. It's also a good idea to scribe this line with a sharp knife, as the pencil line may get rubbed off during the carving process. This "centerline" should actually be offset ½ to ¾ inch to the right side of the stock blank to allow for the cheek piece of the stock (or the reverse for a left-handed shooter).

Make the rough inletting cuts with a Forstner bit in a drill press. Then use a straight chisel to finish the cuts.

Fitting the Action

Now comes the hard part—cutting the stock to receive the action and barrel. Measure the largest portion of the receiver first and locate it lengthwise in relation to the blank. Then, using a caliper or micrometer, measure it and mark this on the top of the blank. Continue measuring and marking the location of the tang, barrel taper, etc. With all the top outside measurements marked, position the blank on the drill press and use a bottoming or Forstner bit to rough-cut for the action, cutting a line of overlapping holes. The rough-cut area then can be cleaned up with a chisel. Measure the depth of the cuts, and use a caliper to set the depth stop on the drill press so you won't drill deeper than you should. Leave the barrel channel alone at this time. The trick to successful inletting in this manner is to start with deepest portions of action and do these first, graduating to the higher portions; for instance, the trigger opening would be the first thing cut. This allows you to drop the action down against the blank to mark for the receiver and tang. Then when this has been cut, it will allow you to mark for the barrel channel, and so on.

Once an area has been cut with the Forstner bit,

it's a matter of chiseling with gouges and straight chisels and even using a small hand grinder to remove the proper amount of wood. Go carefully and continue fitting and measuring as you go. Once you have the recess cut to the point that the action will start to fit down in the blank, you can start using inletting black paint to ensure a proper fit. Coat all metal parts, then drop the action in place. Where the metal touches the wood it will leave a black mark. Remove the wood at this area. This is strictly slow, trial-and-error work. If you remove too much you can't put it back.

If the gun has a one-piece guard and magazine, fit the floorplate in the gun first. You can then use

Opposite and left:
A gouge and chisel can be used
for the final inletting, or use a
small hand grinder for the more
delicate operations. Then use
barrel-inletting tools to shape
barrel channel; a scraper can be
used to put a final smooth finish
on the channel.

the front-tang screw hole of the floorplate as a
guide for locating the action and the barrel.

A 3-inch-long guide pin placed through the front
screw hole of the action, then through the stock
and into the front hole of the floorplate, will locate
the rifle lengthwise properly in regard to the floorplate. Normally when the barrel and action are
dropped in place you will have to remove a bit of
wood for a proper fit to allow the floorplate and
action to line up in the stock. If you're fitting an
Enfield or another type of gun which has a separate guard and magazine, you must fit the magazine first. You can then utilize the magazine box
as a guide to locate the barrel and action.

The most important factor in fitting a rifle action
is the recoil lug. This must be inletted as solidly
and squarely as possible up against the recoil
shoulder of the stock. If this doesn't fit properly you

Mark locations of guard-screw holes and bore to fit. On some guns you may want to install guard first, then action.

will not have an accurate rifle and probably sooner or later the unequal pressure will cause the rifle stock to split.

All stock bolts should go through the stock easily, without binding in any place. The main thing is to have rear tang of the action seated solidly in place against the wood at the rear.

For an accurate rifle, the action should sit solidly on the bottom of the action cuts at two points: around the rear tang screw and on top of the recoil shoulder of the stock near the front stock screw. Other points around the action can fit snugly, but

The fitted action.

should not bind. Where a third or middle stock screw is used, as on the Winchester Model 70, be sure the action is supported around this third stock screw on a proper level with the rear and front screw. If it is not supported with wood at this point, the action can easily be sprung by tightening this screw. When bedding bench-rest rifles, it is a good idea to fit the action equally snugly at either side of the front stock bolt, sides and bottom of receiver ring, and ahead of the front stock bolt to avoid any sideplay of action. Use barrel-inletting gouges, scrapers, etc. to inlet the barrel channel properly, making sure you have it cut to the proper depth.

Bedding the Barrel

With the gun properly inletted, you're ready for the barrel bedding. The reason for bedding a rifle in a solid material such as fiberglass is that it's almost impossible to carve the inletting so the gun will fit like a glove, and you wouldn't want that in any case. The heat of firing has a tendency to cause a gun to warp a bit. Although there is a great deal of controversy over methods of bedding, most gun writers will agree that properly done, barrel bedding will improve the accuracy of the gun, as well as lengthen the life of the stock.

The main thing for a proper bedding job is to ensure that you have it bedded in those portions that take the most amount of recoil, such as around the entire recoil-lug area and around the receiver-ring area. Reinhart Fajen Company suggests that the barrel be bedded by positioning the barrel so it rests equally on two points in the barrel groove at the fore-end tip; each point should be 45° off center from the bottom of the barrel groove. The barrel should not bind in any other portion of the barrel channel. This technique is called a floating barrel bedding.

In some cases, for instance on bench-rest rifles, you may wish to fill the entire magazine-box area with bedding material.

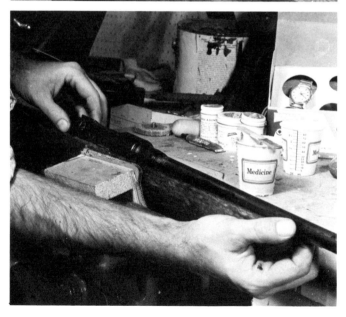

Opposite and left:
For accuracy and proper inletting the action should be bedded in the stock with fiberglass bedding material. Release agent is applied to the barrel. Glass is mixed according to manufacturer's instructions and placed in areas around recoil lug, barrel, etc., then action and barrel are fitted in place. After glass has cured, gently tap action from stock with plastic or rubber mallet.

Inletting screws can be made from the old guard screws to hasten the work if you prefer, or you can purchase them for some model guns. This makes the work of removing and seating the action much easier. Incidentally, you may wish to do the bedding after the outside of the rifle is shaped. This is merely a matter of preference.

The bedding material is purchased in kit form, and make sure you read the instructions properly. The main thing is to make sure you have the entire metal portion of the action and barrel well coated with release agent. If you don't you won't be able to get the action from the stock. Then mix the bedding material according to the manufacturer's instructions and put it in the stock with a small wooden spatula. Then position the action in place, tighten it securely with the guard or inletting screws, and allow the fiberglass to cure for the length of time required by the manufacturer. Remove the action and examine for any bubbles or fill areas that should be reglassed.

Shaping the Stock

Now for the outside. This is the fun part and where you can really show your imagination and woodworking ability. The stock is rough-shaped first by marking the top outline and bandsawing to thin down the fore-end and cut for the cheekpiece. Then place the blank in a solid vise and use sharp chisels and gouges to rough-cut the blank to shape. Continue turning the blank as you carve to make sure you get it symmetrical and balanced properly. When carving, make sure you cut wood in the same direction as the grain runs, or pieces will break out or splinter. Leave the stock a little thick or high where it meets metal parts so you can fine-file or sand these parts down for a good blend of metal to wood. A good cabinetmaker's rasp as well as the Stanley Surform tools can be used to rough

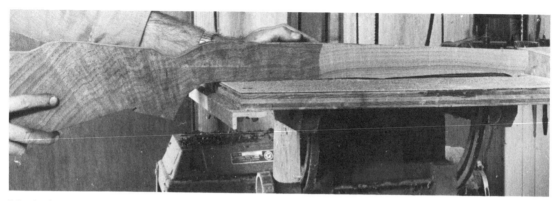

Mark the outline on top of the stock and rough-cut to shape on a bandsaw, then with the blank secured solidly, use carving tools to carve the outside of the blank to shape. Always cut with the grain so you don't knock out chips or splinter the wood. A cabinetmaker's rasp can be used for final shaping.

away the material. When the stock has been partially roughed in, install the buttplate and the pistol-grip bottom as a guide to thickness of these areas. Then file to shape. A barrel-inletting tool can be used to cut the area around the cheekpiece as well as the front portion of the cheekpiece where it overhangs the grip.

When you're satisfied with the stock shape, start sanding. A flap sander in a portable electric drill will help a great deal during the rough sanding.

Fit buttplate and pistol-grip bottom in place, then final-shape to suit.

Then use progressively finer grits of sandpaper to sand the stock properly. Finish and checker stock as desired.

You can also add more embellishments to the stock—different types of wood for the fore-end, such as ebony or zebrawood, or wood inlays in the stock as well.

The stock can be rough-sanded using a flap sander in a power drill. Then follow with progressively finer grits of sandpaper to sand as smooth as possible, taking out last marks of coarser sandpaper with fine finishing paper.

For a really deluxe appearance, bolt should be jeweled using a jeweling jig on the drill press.

You can also alter the bolt handle to suit. Shown are a couple of replacement handles that can be welded on the bolt.

Metalwork

With the stock finished, you're ready for the metalwork. Install new sights as desired. The gun shown has a front ramp and sight and a Williams Receiver sight, the ramp installed by silver-soldering and the receiver sight by drilling and tapping. Touch up metal bluing as needed, or you can reblue if necessary.

One of the most impressive things you can do is to jewel the bolt. For this you will need a bolt-jeweling jig, jeweling brushes, and grinding compound. Incidentally, this is one job that drives me up the wall because it seems to take forever and is too much like standing on a factory line. The way I like to do it is set the job up on the drill press and leave it all day. Every time I pass by the machine, I do a couple of lines, then quit and go on to something else.

You may also wish to add a more decorative bolt, and in many cases you will have to alter the bolt handle by bending or welding to allow the use of a scope on the rifle.

Adding sling swivels and a sling will also add a great deal to the rifle. Other additions can also include checkering the bolt handle, or adding a larger safety or trigger shoe, a Schnaubel front end, or even cutting down or trimming down the trigger guard on Mauser-style guns.

Installing sling swivels is an easy chore that can give a "customizing" touch to almost any gun. Shown is Brownell's Quick Set Latigo sling that can be quickly adjusted for carrying or shooting.

APPENDIX

GUNSMITHING SUPPLIES AND GUN PARTS COMPANIES

Birchwood Casey
7900 Fuller Road
Eden Prairie, Minn. 55343

E. C. Bishop & Son, Inc.
Box 7
Warsaw, Mo. 65355

Bonanza Sports, Mfg.
412-1 Western Ave.
Faribault, MN 55021

Brownell's Inc.
Route 2, Box 1
Montezuma, Iowa 50171

B-Square Company
Box 11281
Ft. Worth, Tx 76109

Bushnell Optical Company
2828 East Foothill Blvd.
Pasadena, Calif. 91107

Century Arms, Inc.
5 Federal Street
St. Albans, Vermont 05478

Chapman Manufacturing Company
Route 17
Durham, Conn. 06422

Federal Firearms Inc.
P. O. Box 145
Oakdale, Penn. 15071

Gunline Tools
719 North East Street
Anaheim, Calif. 92805

Herter's Inc.
Waseca,
Minnesota 56093

Hodgdon Powder Company
Shawnee Mission,
Kansas 66202

Jason/Empire, Inc.
9200 Cody, P. O. Box 12370
Overland Park, Ks. 66212

Jet Aer Corp.
Paterson
New Jersey 07524

Leupold-Nosler
P. O. Box 688
Beaverton, OR 97005

Lyman Products
Route 147
Middlefield, Ct. 06455

Marble Arms Corp.
1009 Industrial Park, P. O. Box
   111
Gladstone, Mich. 49837

Frank Mittermeier, Inc.
3577 E. Tremont Ave.
Bronx, N. Y. 10465

Numrich Arms Corp.
West Hurley
New York 12491

Poly-Choke
933 Tunxis St.
Hartford, Conn. 06101

Redfield
5800 East Jewell Ave.
Denver, Colo. 80224

Reinhart Fajen Inc.
Box 338
Warsaw, Mo. 65355

Sherwood Distributors, Inc.
18714 Parthenia Street
Northridge, Calif. 91324

Simmons Gun Specialties Inc.
700 Rogers Road
Olathe, Ks. 66061

Swift Instruments
952 Dorchester Ave.
Boston, Mass. 02125

Tasco
1075 N. W. 71st St.
Miami, Florida 33138

W. R. Weaver Company
El Paso
Texas 79915

Williams Gun Sight Company
7389 Lapeer Road
Davison, Michigan 48423

GUN MANUFACTURERS

Beeman's Precision Airguns, Inc.
47 Paul Drive
San Rafael, Ca. 94903

Benjamin Air Rifle Co.
807 Marion Street
St. Louis, Mo. 63104

The Beretta Arms Company, Inc.
P. O. Box 2000
Ridgefield, Conn. 06877

Browning
Morgan,
Utah 84050

Charter Arms Corp.
430 Sniffens Lane
Stratford, Conn. 06497

Colt Firearms Division
150 Hyshope Ave.
Hartford, Conn. 06102

Connecticut Valley Arms, Inc.
Saybrook Road
Haddam, Ct. 06438

Crossman Arms Company
980 Turk Hill Road
Fairport, N. Y. 14450

Dixie Gun Works
Hwy 51 South
Union City, Tenn. 38261

J. L. Galef & Sons, Inc.
85 Chambers Street
New York, N. Y. 10007

Golden Eagle Firearms, Inc.
P. O. Box 42139, 5700 Ranchester
Houston Tx. 77042

Harrington & Richardson, Inc.
Industrial Row
Gardner, Mass. 01440

Ithaca Gun Company, Inc.
Terrace Hill
Ithaca, N. Y. 14850

The Marlin Firearms Company
100 Kenna Drive
North Haven, Conn. 06473

O. F. Mossberg & Sons, Inc.
7 Grasso Ave.
North Haven, Conn. 06473

Power Line Division
Victor Comptometer Corp.
Box 220
Rogers, Ark. 72756

Remington Arms Company, Inc.
Bridgeport,
Conn. 06602

Savage Arms Division,
Emhart Industries, Inc.
Westfield, Mass. 01085

Sheridan Products, Inc.
3205 Sheridan Road
Racine, Wisc. 54403

SKB Sports, Inc.
190 Shepard Ave.
Wheeling, Il. 60090

Smith & Wesson
2100 Roosevelt Ave.
Springfield, Ma. 01101

Stoeger Industries
55 Ruta Court
South Hackensack, N. J. 07606

Sturm, Ruger & Company Inc.
Southport,
Conn. 06480

Thompson/Center Arms
Farmington Road
Rochester, New Hampshire 03867

Weatherby Firearms
2781 E. Firestone Blvd.
South Gate, Calif. 91280

Dan Wesson Arms, Inc.
293 Main Street
Monson, Ma. 01057

Winchester-Western
275 Winchester Ave.
New Haven, Conn. 06504

INDEX

(boldface numbers refer to illustrations)